KNOWLEDGE REVIEW

Teaching and learning communication skills in social work education

Pamela Trevithick, Sally Richards, Gillian Ruch and Bernard Moss

With Linda Lines and Oded Manor

Social Care Institute for Excellence

Better knowledge for better practice

The POLICY PRESS

swap *ltsn*

Social Policy and Social Work
Learning and Teaching Support Network

First published in Great Britain in May 2004 by the Social Care Institute for Excellence (SCIE)

Social Care Institute for Excellence
1st Floor
Goldings House
2 Hay's Lane
London SE1 2HB
UK
www.scie.org.uk

British Library Cataloguing in Publication Data

A catalogue record for this book is available from the British Library

ISBN 1 904812 12 0

Pamela Trevithick is Senior Lecturer in the School for Policy Studies at the University of Bristol. **Sally Richards** is a Lecturer in the School of Health and Social Care at the University of Reading. **Gillian Ruch** is a Lecturer in the Division of Social Work Studies at the University of Southampton. **Bernard Moss** is a Principal Lecturer in Social Work and Applied Studies and a Learning and Teaching Fellow at Staffordshire University.

Linda Lines is a Lecturer in Work-based Learning in the Department of Social Work at the Open University. **Oded Manor** is an Independent Groupwork Consultant, formerly Principal Lecturer in Social Work, Middlesex University.

Produced by The Policy Press
University of Bristol
Fourth Floor, Beacon House
Queen's Road
Bristol BS8 1QU
UK
www.policypress.org.uk

Front cover: photograph supplied by kind permission of third-avenue.co.uk
Printed and bound in Great Britain by Hobbs the Printers Ltd, Southampton.

Contents

Preface

This review is one of a series supporting the introduction of a new degree in social work. Teaching and learning of communication skills is a core social work skill, and this review assists social work educators and students by examining the different approaches underpinning this critical aspect of social work education. The review will contribute to a *resource guide* for social work educators and students, to be made available early summer 2004. We are grateful to the authors for undertaking this review, and also to the Social Policy and Social Work Learning and Teaching Support Network (SWAPltsn) for their support and assistance as co-commissioners of this work.

Other reviews in this series will focus on the teaching and learning of assessment, of law in social work, of partnership working, of interprofessional working and of human growth and behaviour.

The review focuses specifically on the teaching and learning of communications skills for those working in the field of social care. Further work is also planned to examine the literature on teaching and learning of communication skills in other sectors such as medicine, nursing and allied health professionals, improving the communications skills of users and also on communication with children.

Wendy Hardyman
Research Analyst

Acknowledgements

The authors would like to extend their appreciation to Julia Phillips (SWAPltsn) for her efficient and sensitive management of the project, and her keen sense of humour, Jackie Rafferty (SWAPltsn) for her incisive comments on the final draft and SCIE staff for the support and guidance provided throughout the review. We would also like to acknowledge the skilful work undertaken by Gill Ritchie, Mark Rodgers and Lisa Jones at the Centre for Reviews and Dissemination, University of York.

Executive summary

- This review of the literature on the learning and teaching of communication skills in social work education was commissioned by the Social Care Institute for Excellence (SCIE), in collaboration with the Social Work and Social Policy Learning and Teaching Support Network (SWAPltsn).

- The context for the review is the introduction of the new social work degree. Underpinning this new award are the National Occupational Standards and Key Skills for Social Work, the Quality Assurance Agency Subject Benchmarks for Social Work, the Department of Health *Requirements for social work training* issued in 2002 and the National Assembly for Wales (NAW) *Requirements for an award of a degree in social work*, issued in 2003. Throughout, there is an emphasis on the importance of communication skills for social work.

- The purpose of the review was:
  - to identify the key messages concerning the learning and teaching of communication skills on social work qualifying courses/training programmes, in order to facilitate effective practice with a range of client groups; and
  - to enable social work educators to reflect these messages in the design and delivery of social work programmes.

- A search of electronic databases was conducted by the Centre for Reviews and Dissemination (CRD) at the University of York using search terms agreed by the Working Group. This generated a vast literature of 8,023 records, mostly relating to communication skills for health professionals. Only records relating to the learning and teaching of communication skills for social care professionals were included in the review, with additional material identified by hand searching key journals and from group members' personal libraries.

- The review focused on two main areas:
  - the theoretical underpinnings for the learning and teaching of communication skills;
  - how communication skills are being taught and to what effect.

Findings

- Much of the literature was from North America and may not be relevant to the UK. Relatively little has been published in the UK on the learning and teaching of communication skills in social work education.
- The review revealed the absence of a common language in the area of communication skills. Terms such as 'interpersonal skills', 'listening skills', 'interviewing skills', 'helping skills', 'counselling skills' and 'micro-skills' were used, but often without careful definition.
- The papers tended to draw on either humanistic psychology and counselling theory, or on communication and learning theory. The link between theory and practice is often tenuous and there is a lack of evidence of any coherent theoretical framework that informs the learning and teaching of communication skills. Theoretical coverage tends to be implicit or, if explicit, lacks depth and critical analysis.
- Most of the training programmes described focused on developing empathy, although micro-skills training, which is concerned with the process of communication, was also in evidence. Recent examples were found of innovative approaches to the learning and teaching of communication skills in social work education in the UK. These attempt to link theory and practice more effectively and to create a suitable learning environment for skill development.
- IT and multi-media based resources are increasingly used in communication skills training. The limited evidence available suggests that they are best used to support, enhance and consolidate – not replace – face-to-face teaching.
- There is little evidence that communication skills training includes either written communication skills or specialist skills for work with children or adults with particular communication needs.
- The findings from evaluative studies suggest that communication skills training generally increases skilfulness and is well received by students. However, improvements do not necessarily transfer to practice settings with service users, which indicates the importance of integrating communication skills training with practice learning.
- The systematic evaluation of communication skills training presents substantial methodological difficulties. A particular challenge is the definition and measurement of outcomes, which typically are measured in terms of changes in the student rather than in service users.

Introduction

Good communication is at the heart of best practice in social work. Indeed, social work was one of the first professions to recognise the importance of communications skills and how these skills link to effective practice[1-4]. It is through our capacity to communicate that we relate and convey our respect and concern for others[5]. Communication skills are also essential to the task of assessment and later decision making, not only for social workers but also for other professionals, particularly those working in the field of health and social care. The importance of communication skills can also be seen in government policy, and the emphasis being placed on the role of service users and carers in relation to the new social work degree, and patients (consumers) in relation to health research, policy and practice. For all professions, the failure to communicate effectively can lead to serious – and sometimes tragic – consequences. In relation to social work, these failures have been been brought to light in the public inquiries into the death of children known to social services[6-8], the most recent tragedy being the death of Victoria Climbié[9]. Poor communication among professionals – and in relation to service users – is one failure that has been highlighted in many of these reports.

These events form part of the background to this knowledge review. Another important influence has been the development of the new degree in social work, implemented by the Department of Health (DH) and the National Assembly for Wales (NAW). With funding made available from the DH and NAW, the Social Care Institute for Excellence (SCIE), in collaboration with the Social Work and Social Policy Learning and Teaching Support Network (SWAPltsn), agreed to commission a Working Group to undertake a research review. The task of the Working Group was to undertake a review of the literature on the learning and teaching of communication skills in social work education, in order to:

- identify the key messages concerning the learning and teaching of communication skills on social work qualifying course/training

programmes, in order to facilitate effective practice with a range of client groups; and
• enable social work educators to reflect these messages in the design and delivery of social work programmes.

Although the work most closely relates to the DH identification of communication as one of the core skills, this knowledge review is also relevant to Wales, in that communication skills form part of the requirements laid down by the Care Council for Wales (CCW).

1.1. The new social work degree

The new degree provides an important context and a strong impetus for this knowledge review because of the emphasis placed on communication skills in the new curriculum. For example, communication skills are a prominent theme in each of the strands that contributes to curriculum development:

• *The national occupational standards*[10] and Key Skills for Social Work defines the competences required for the social work role.
• The Quality Assurance Agency benchmark statement[11] places the education and training of social workers firmly in the context of the learning outcomes and academic standards expected at degree level.
• The *Requirements for social work training*[12] lays down entry requirements for candidates applying for social work courses, and clear teaching, learning and assessment standards. The document also identifies five key areas, one of which is "communication skills with children, adults and those with particular communication needs"[13]. The requirements for Wales also place great emphasis on effective communication.
• The Care Councils (General Social Care Council [GSCC], Care Council for Wales [CCW]), whose roles are to monitor the quality of social work education, have a strong emphasis on students' 'fitness for practice'. This inevitably includes the quality of students' communication skills and how these are used in all aspects of their social work practice.
• Additional funding has been made available to social work programmes to establish skills laboratories to help students develop their communication skills in ways that are effective and transferable.

As part of the *Requirements for social work training* put forward by the Care Councils, the emphasis in the new degree is not only on improving interprofessional communication but improving communication skills with service users. Pierson and Thomas[14] highlight the importance of communication in social work in relation to service users, and also with regard to others involved in practice effectiveness and 'high quality results':

> In social work and social welfare agencies, good, clear, accurate communication is essential in several contexts. First, all organisations should provide quality information about services that they offer, which should be widely accessible. This will involve not only a range of languages relevant to their local community, but also in electronic, Braille and perhaps taped formats.
>
> Secondly, all workers need to develop appropriate communication skills both for face-to-face and for written communications. The ability to avoid jargon and to communicate in good, clear English or Welsh is of paramount importance. When using other languages, it is equally important that the clear meaning is fully communicated. Workers also need to consider the context in which they are required to speak and to write, and to ensure that they develop a style that is appropriate and relevant for their audience.
>
> Thirdly, some people have specific communication needs. People who take pride in belonging to the deaf community, for example, need to be offered trained competent British Sign Language (BSL) interpreters so that they can communicate clearly in their first language. Some people who have serious communication problems as a result of disability may require specialist support for communication (see Braille, low-vision aids, Moon).
>
> Fourthly, agencies that are closely collaborating on projects, working in partnership or negotiating service level agreements, need to develop effective channels for communication in order to enhance collaboration.
>
> Fifthly, with the developing emphasis upon a research culture in social welfare, workers need to be able to communicate clearly with funders, research colleagues and research participants in order to produce high

quality results and be able to disseminate their findings clearly and imaginatively in order to improve practice.

Finally, communication has a non-verbal dimension. Workers need to be aware of body language, and the importance of listening skills, as part of their effective communication repertoire.[14]

1.2. The Working Group and preparation of the review

An invitation to apply to join a Working Group to write a review of the literature on the learning and teaching of communication skills in social work education was issued by SCIE/SWAPltsn in March 2003. From a wide range of people who expressed an interest in undertaking this task, six social work educators were selected to join the Working Group. All had experience of teaching communication skills, together with research knowledge in this field. In addition, the Working Group included a member of SWAPltsn who acted as a resource to the group. Representatives from SCIE were also involved with the Working Group in their role as commissioners, and also in relation to circulating papers and articles identified as relevant to the literature search and review.

The process of identifying the literature for inclusion in the research review proved challenging. There exists a vast literature on communication skills, most of which related to the health professions. Some preliminary searching conducted by a research analyst at SCIE identified key literature and the utility of various search terms. These details, together with examples of relevant records, identified from preliminary searching, were passed on to the Centre for Reviews and Dissemination (CRD) at the University of York, who were commissioned to undertake an electronic database search. (See **Appendix A** for a more detailed account of the search strategy adopted.) Hand searching of selected journals produced further material, and the Working Group also drew on books and articles from their own personal libraries.

Given the extensive literature on communication skills, determining the scope of the search presented some difficulties. It was anticipated that the literature in this area relating specifically to social work might be quite limited. At the same time, it was felt that the literature from professions outside of social work and social care, such as nursing, medicine and allied professions, was likely to be relevant to social work. In time it became clear that the limited time and resources available for this task meant that it was only possible for the knowledge review to focus on those areas most relevant to the new degree. For this reason, it was agreed to focus on those records relating to the learning and teaching of communication skills for social care professionals. As part of the selection process, two group members read and coded all abstracts considered to be relevant under four headings: theoretical, narrative, evaluative, and specialist communication skills. These categories enabled the Working Group to explore the extent to which theoretical knowledge underpins the learning and teaching of communication skills. They also allowed a focus to be placed on how communication skills are being taught on social work courses, and to what effect. Working collaboratively in pairs, group members prepared a draft report. This was submitted to two independent reviewers, and the DH and NAW, for their comments. The completed report has benefited from the reviewers' observations and recommendations.

The next chapter outlines the methodology used. This is followed by the findings from the literature review which address four main questions:

- What theoretical frameworks inform the learning and teaching of communication skills?
- How have social work teachers designed and implemented programmes for learning communication skills?
- What has been the impact, if any, of learning communication skills?
- What is known about the learning and teaching of specialist communication skills?

The knowledge review concludes with key messages and suggestions for further work.

Methodology

The focus of the knowledge review was on learning and teaching of communication skills in social work education. Most of the literature used in the review came from a search of electronic databases. In addition, hand searching of key journals was undertaken and further references added from the Working Group's own personal libraries. This was a key source for texts.

2.1. Electronic databases

The electronic database search undertaken by CRD at the University of York looked at bibliographic databases covering social work, social sciences and health literature. These were searched over a two-week period, between 12/03/03 and 03/04/03. (See **Appendix A,** Table 1.) The strategy was developed using Sociological Abstracts and MEDLINE databases. No language limits were applied. However, literature published before 1982 was excluded. It was felt that this literature was not likely to be relevant to the current context of social work, and the changes that have taken place in social work education over the last 20 years.

2.2. Hand searching

CRD provided a frequency distribution of the journals in which records identified as relevant were published. A decision was made to search electronically available online contents (abstracts and papers) from January 2002 to the present day for the 10 most frequently cited journals. (For details of the journals searched, see **Appendix A,** Table 2.)

2.3. Authors' personal libraries/preliminary scoping

In addition to the records identified from the electronic search, texts and journal papers were also identified from the authors' personal libraries.

2.4. Inclusion criteria

The electronic database search generated 8,023 records of possible relevance to this review. The number of records retrieved was the result of the decision to widen the search to include the health-related literature. As it was impossible to investigate and report on such a vast literature within the time available, it was decided to include in the review only those records deemed of primary relevance – those about improving the communication skills of social care professionals, through learning and teaching of communications skills. In order to identify these records a coding strategy was developed. This also enabled the literature generated from the electronic database search to be mapped. (See **Appendix A**, 'Preliminary coding and inclusion criteria', and Figure 1 for further details.)

2.5. Data recording and quality appraisal

All papers included in the review were subject to data quality appraisal. Information and quality appraisal of these papers was recorded using a predetermined format. (See also **Appendix A**, 'Data recording and quality appraisal'.)

2.6. Results

Of the 8,023 records generated from the electronic database search, 150 records met the inclusion criteria. The majority of these were retrieved from the database 'Social Work Abstracts'.

Following a two-stage process for assessing the relevance of these records, the total number included in the review from the electronic search totalled 59 (45 papers and 14 texts). A further 4 papers were identified through hand searching, of which 2 were included in the review process and an additional 20 texts, 1 report, 3 journal papers (1 of these from a preliminary scoping exercise) and 1 e-learning package from authors' personal libraries. (See **Appendix A**, 'Results' and Figure 2, for a detailed write-up of results.)

The total number of records included in this review from the various search strategies was 86 records – 50 papers, 34 texts, 1 report and 1 e-learning package[5,12,15-98].

There were 10 texts, not included in the numbers above or in the main body of the review, that authors identified from their personal libraries as useful for further additional reading[1,2,4,99-105].

3

Theoretical frameworks underpinning the learning and teaching of communication skills

From data identified in the York electronic database literature search, only 16 papers were identified as being relevant in their coverage of the theoretical frameworks informing the learning and teaching of communication skills in social work education – and many of these papers were quite dated. In some papers, the theoretical coverage tends to be implicit or, if explicit, tends to lack sufficient depth and critical analysis. There may be two reasons for this limited coverage of theory. First, it may suggest that some authors do not consider it necessary to provide a detailed theoretical exploration, perhaps because it is assumed that most readers will know and understand the theoretical assumptions that underpin their work. This assumption may be correct for social work academics but one that calls for caution in relation to social work students and practitioners. Second, it may suggest that some authors believe that an exploration of theory is not necessary in relation to skills learning and teaching. Whatever the reason, the underlying assumptions that inform many of the papers imply that it is possible to be an effective communicator without an explicit knowledge of theory. We would argue with this assumption. Of the texts mentioned in this knowledge review, some were identified in the York search. These – and other texts – are covered later in this chapter.

In relation to the link between theory and practice, there were some papers that attempt to address this issue. For example, 2 papers[36,60] and 1 book chapter[54] look at the application of specific theories to the task of learning and teaching. Two further papers also attempt to link theory and practice in this way, but in areas that are more specialised[47,69]. The paper by Dickson and Bamford[30] is particularly impressive in its detailed overview of key issues in relation to learning and teaching of communication skills in social work education in the UK. Dickson and Bamford[30] comment on the lack of research and publications on this subject, which they broaden to include all publications relating to interpersonal skills:

> Interpersonal skills which enable the worker to engage meaningfully with the client, lie at the heart of effective social work practice ... it is, perhaps, surprising that relatively little has been published by way of a systematic exploration of current social work education/training provision in promoting skilled professional interaction.[106]

The few articles on this subject identified in the CRD search seem to support this view. However, some difficulties may be due to differences in terminology. Dickson and Bamford are a case in point. Although these authors use the term *interpersonal skills* in their paper, they are, in effect, writing about communication skills. The same is true of some texts, such as Hargie et al[51]. In other papers, *interviewing skills* is the preferred term. The use of different terms highlights a difficulty regularly encountered in the papers reviewed – and in social work generally – which is that we do not share a common language. In order to address this problem of terminology, and the absence of clear definitions, it was agreed to add a glossary of terms to this knowledge review. (See **Appendix C**.)

Similarly, there is little conformity in the range of approaches used to teach social work skills. Some appear to adopt quite different teaching methods, but with little reference to theory. These findings support research where newly qualified social work/probation practitioners were asked to name those theories they found useful, and were still using in their work. Over 80 theorists and theoretical approaches were identified from this question[107]. These findings highlight the diversity of theories and methods taught, or learnt, on social work courses and the confusion that existed among the practitioners interviewed about what constitutes a theoretical approach. The seven main models included: Rogerian and other counselling approaches; task-centred social work; systemic ideas influencing especially family work/therapy; behavioural techniques; child development mainly based on Erikson's stages; psycho-social approaches; and crisis intervention[108]. These findings are also in keeping with the emphasis on psychological perspectives found in the 16 papers read in this chapter.

This level of diversity makes it hard to conceptualise similarities and differences, and strengths and limitations, of the different approaches adopted – a point taken up by Koprowska, who noted that: "The process of professional learning in the wider field is not fully understood; empirical studies are rare and methodological differences make comparison difficult"[109]. It also makes it difficult to identify whether the transfer of learning into – and across – different practice contexts has been effective.

A further drawback relates to the international flavour of the papers reviewed. Ten of the 16 articles reviewed describe the situation in North America[16,21,24,27,36,47,53,65,70,93], with only 3 articles referring to the UK[30,60,69]. The remaining 3 papers relate to the educational context in Israel[23], to skills teaching in Germany[61] and the international context from a Norwegian perspective[90]. For these reasons, it has not been possible to draw any firm conclusions for England, and we suspect the same is true for Wales, Scotland and Northern Ireland.

Overall, psychological theories feature strongly in the papers reviewed. Humanistic psychology, informed by the client-centred theories of Carl Rogers[83,84], and psychosocial theories influenced by Freudian psychoanalytic theory, are the most commonly referenced theories. Where social work texts are cited, these references also reflect a more psychological perspective. Some authors attempt to redress this imbalance, calling for greater focus to be placed on social factors, such as "social development"[110], or argue that there is a 'dissonance' when technical skills are taught within "humanist principles, without reference to any political context"[111]. These limitations withstanding, it is possible to group the papers into three general sections: psychology and counselling theory; communication and learning theory; and other theoretical perspectives.

3.1. Psychology and counselling theory

Much of the literature reviewed draws heavily on humanistic psychology and counselling theory. For example, several papers cite Carl Rogers and sometimes also Carkhuff[16,23,27,53,70,93]. The influence of counselling can be seen in many of the texts cited in the articles reviewed. Hepworth and Larsden[112] are cited in a range of papers[16,23,27,30], mainly because, it is argued, these authors "frame their analysis on an updated version of the Rogerian core conditions: empathy, authenticity, and respect"[23]. Fischer[42,43] is also cited, largely for his teaching and writing on 'micro-skills', including empathy[24,27,93]. The focus placed on empathy is interesting, and may reflect the fact that empathy is important in counselling, as well as social work. Perhaps for this reason, this has led to a number of research studies on the effectiveness of empathy training in social work education[113]. The work of Egan (the most recent edition of his text is cited here, as there are seven editions of the book)[37] and his model of Problem Management and Opportunity Development, which is firmly located in the field of counselling theory, is also cited in several places and not always uncritically[21,54,60].

There is little attempt to analyse why humanistic psychology, particularly the work of Carl Rogers, is popular among social work students and practitioners. Similarly, there is little attempt to analyse critically the relevance of counselling theory to social work. As a result, insufficient attention is paid to the difficulties inherent when trying to apply concepts such as empathy to fieldwork settings, particularly statutory social work. It is again important to note that much of the literature referred to is more influential in North America than the UK.

3.2. Communication and learning theory

Under this heading are grouped references to communication and learning theory[30,47,60], with several authors referencing the work of Hargie[50]. Communication theory draws on the principles of motor skills and transfers them into the context of social and communication skills. This perspective emphasises the 'technical' activity involved in communication. The particular importance of communication theory is its focus on 'micro-skills' that is, on the process of communication and the actual skills used in practice, but again, this theory draws heavily on psychology and counselling. For this reason, the skills it addresses are sometimes called 'micro-counselling' skills. One tension that arises from relying on communication theory is that it tends to see effective communication as a personal trait. Once a person has acquired this competence, it travels with that individual across different situations. However, it is argued that "researchers have demonstrated that the ability to communicate competently is largely dependent on social context"[114], as well as personal competence. If competence is context-specific in this way, this makes any analysis of competence and the transferability of skills a more complex issue than first assumed.

Learning theory and principles of behaviourism – assessment, evaluation, feedback and reinforcement – feature in the literature as useful theoretical tools for facilitating the process of skills acquisition[26]. Interestingly, adult learning theory[58,86] focusing on experiential learning and the concept of 'learning by doing' – which might have been expected to inform the teaching of communication skills – is referenced in only 2 papers[47,60]. Hansen explores 'learning by doing' and Schön's[86,87] notions of 'reflection-in-action' in relation to the use of video in skills teaching. Koprowska, taking up some of the points made by Hansen, draws on a quote from Schön:

> Perhaps, then, learning all forms of professional artistry depends, at least in part, on conditions similar to those created in the studios and conservatories: freedom to learn by doing in a setting relatively low in risk, with access to coaches who initiate students into the 'traditions of the calling' and help them, by 'the right kind of telling', to see on their own behalf and in their own way what they most need to see'.[116]

3.3. Other theoretical perspectives

Another group of papers, written more recently, provide very clear and accessible accounts of specific theoretical frameworks and their application in practice[36,54,60,61]. Edwards and Richards, Jessup and Rogerson and Koprowska warrant specific mention.

Edwards and Richards[36] write on the application of 'relational/cultural theory' to learning and teaching in social work education. Based on the work of Jean Baker Miller and Janet Stiver[117], and others involved in the Stone Centre in Boston, US[55], their paper describes a psychosocial, relational perspective with regard to concepts such as mutual engagement, empathy and mutual empowerment. The paper argues that these concepts are not only important in the client–worker relationship but also in the student–teacher relationship:

> We believe that growth in social work education is the result of the student and teacher experiencing the dynamics of empowerment that come with mutual empathy.[118]

This perspective states that how students are taught will influence what they learn, and that this in turn will influence how they use this knowledge and understanding in practice.

The chapter by Jessup and Rogerson[54] describes a postmodern and poststructural approach to teaching and practising interpersonal communication skills, arguing the case for teaching to be located in a 'political context'. Drawing on the work of Foucault[119], Freire[44], and Freire and Shor[45], concepts such as language and power are defined within this theoretical framework, and then applied to 'explicitly targeted exercises' to highlight their use in practice. The paper argues that certain concepts, such as those based on humanist principles, "have been constructed to produce an oppressive, rather than a liberating, social work practice"[120]. The authors argue for an alternative "discourse and practice", which "coherently address the primary concern of our profession: personal and social change"[120].

Koprowska's article[60] provides an overview of the skills training in social work education, both within universities and in practice settings. In a complex paper, Koprowska explores 'key concepts and methods' in relation to Agazarian's theory of 'living human systems', particularly 'systems–centred therapy', and how this process of learning and teaching can be applied within social work education. According to Koprowska, systems–centred therapy "deliberately structures group norms in order to reduce restraining forces and increase driving forces"[121]. The part played by 'predictable defences' needs to be 'undone' so that new information can be integrated in ways that enable students to "move away from personal preoccupations toward a process of professional discovery"[122].

In addition, two other papers warrant mention. The first, by Hansen[47], provides an account of the work of Schön and Dreyfus and Dreyfus[123] on direct skills acquisition, and how these theories can be used in teaching, with particular reference to the use of 'interactive video' as an 'instructional technology'[124]. The second paper, by McMahon[69], is based on psychoanalytic theory and describes the application of these theories developed by Winnicott[125-7] and Dockar-Drysdale[128] to 'therapeutic communication' with children and young people.

No papers were identified that provided a commentary on how students view and experience the different models of teaching in relation to communication skills, or their preferences. Similarly, although Bricker-Jenkins[21] and Lishman[62] call for service users to be "considered the primary experts"[129], no papers explored the views of services users or carers on the competence of students and social work practitioners in relation to their communication skills. It is likely that this gap will be addressed in the requirements for the new social work degree[12,130].

Some papers touched on the transferability of skills from the classroom or 'laboratory' to practice settings, and between different client groups, settings and contexts[24,90]. On the whole, this subject is not explored in great detail – an issue that is mentioned in the Brunel Practice Survey – "transferability of core learning is often assumed and opportunities for drawing this learning out were scarce"[131]. One exception is the article by Dickson and Bamford[132], who attempt to look at the "broader principles governing action". These authors call for greater crossover in terms of the design and delivery of social work (interpersonal) skills teaching.

3.4. Texts covering communication skills

Our findings revealed that of the 14 texts identified in the CRD electronic database search, only 2 references had social work in their title: *Requirements for social work training*[12] and *The social work skills workbook*[28]. Other texts identified as relevant to social work were targeted toward health professions[22,26,29,37,38,50,75], or covered more specialist areas, such as counselling or interviewing skills[32,40] or communication skills in specific contexts[15,46,97]. Of these texts, Collins and Collins[26] *Social skills training and the professional helper* and Cournoyer[28] *The social work skills workbook* have particular relevance to the learning and teaching of communication skills in social work. However, the tendency to target texts toward a more multi-professional readership made it difficult to assess the relevance of certain texts to social work.

However, from our knowledge and experience as academics, it was clear that more coverage of communication skills learning and teaching could be found in other textbooks than the limited number identified in the York electronic database search. As a result, we agreed to hand search key social work texts, using the same criteria adopted in the York search. Time restraints did not allow this search to be extensive but it highlighted some important texts[62,81] and chapters[54]. Lishman's[62] *Communication in social work* is the only book included in the main body of the review that explicitly mentions both communication skills and social work in its title. Other texts provide considerable coverage of communication skills, such as Kadushin and Kadushin[56], Thompson[92] and Trevithick[94], while others focus on specific approaches to practice, such as counselling[88]. Thompson[92] provides a valuable account of the importance of verbal and non-verbal communication skills, and also writing and interviewing skills. A third range of generalist texts have specific sections dedicated to communication skills[133], and a fourth category located in our search focused on the importance of writing and presentation skills[92].

3.5. Summary of theoretical concerns

It has proved difficult to identify a coherent theoretical framework that informs the learning and teaching of communication skills in social work. The tenuous relationship between theory and practice in relation to social work skills, including communication skills, means that practitioners have tended to look to other theories outside social work to help them to understand human beings, and to acquire advanced or specialist skills[134]. Counselling theory and practice is particularly attractive in this regard, with its specific and accessible terminology. A closer relationship between theory and practice, linked to research, particularly in relation to learning and teaching communication skills, is a crucially important issue, and one that will no doubt be addressed in some detail in relation to the new social work degree.

4

Teaching and learning communication skills: a review of the evidence

We turn next to review the literature relating to the second and third of our four central questions:

- How have social work teachers designed and implemented programmes for learning communication skills?
- What impact, if any, have such programmes had?

The literature containing evidence on the content and effectiveness of communication skills training in social work education substantially overlaps the literature reviewed above. It has similar limitations, in particular the lack of a coherent body of evidence on which to draw and the preponderance of work from North America. By comparison the literature specific to the UK appears somewhat meagre.

The evidence can be grouped under two main headings. *Narrative accounts* provide detailed descriptions of the design and content of skills training programmes, with no attempt at systematic evaluation. *Evaluative accounts* typically contain a more limited description of programme content and rationale, focusing instead on the measurement of outcomes. The literature that deals with the recent surge in the use of computer-aided learning (CAL) has tended to include an evaluative dimension to it, although the successful transferability of the transatlantic experience to the UK context is by no means guaranteed.

One further point deserves emphasis. In the narrative and evaluative literature identified in this review there was a notable absence of any reference to training students in *written* communication skills. The importance of this area of work cannot be denied, and points to the need for further work to be undertaken. This crucial limitation to the scope of this study is admitted at the outset.

4.1. Design and implementation

Taken together, the narrative and evaluative accounts give an overview of different approaches to the learning and teaching of communication skills. The programmes described vary in length and intensity and involve students at different stages of undergraduate or postgraduate social work courses. Most focus on the development of basic interpersonal skills in interviewing and combine formal input from an instructor with experiential learning, usually in small group sessions with role-play and video. Behavioural methods are widely used, with systematic feedback and reinforcement provided by tutors or peers. In the earlier literature, the training programmes focus on developing empathic communication – the ability to grasp the meaning of communication in terms of content and affect and to respond appropriately. Micro-skills training, with its emphasis on the processes of communication, is prominent in the more recent literature.

The programmes that focus on empathy share a common theoretical basis in the work of Carl Rogers, Carkhuff and other counselling theorists. However, substantial variation is apparent in the content of individual programmes. For example, Toseland and Spielberg[135] focus on the skills required to "facilitate client self-exploration and action: empathy; genuineness; respect; concreteness; confrontation; self-disclosure; warmth; immediacy; potency and self-actualisation". Nerdrum and Lundquist[74] work with their students on: tuning in; decentering; active listening; empathic communication; confrontation and understanding of client resistance[136]. Nerdrum and Lundquist's thoughtful and relatively recent article is also an indication that the empathy-based approach to skills training continues to develop. Bondareva et al[18] provides another recent example of professional training that is directed towards developing the personality of the social work student, but with limited information about programme content and method. Non-behavioural approaches to developing empathy, such as structured meditation[57] and experiential focusing[27], that aim to increase the student's perceptual awareness, are found only in the earlier literature.

Micro-skills training, which is concerned with improving the student's mastery of the processes of communication, offers an alternative highly structured approach. Dickson and Mullan[31] describe sessions on each of the seven interviewing skills: non-verbal communication; questioning; reflecting; listening; explaining; set induction and closure[137]. This approach is particularly associated in the UK with the work of Hargie and colleagues[50,51].

While the evaluative literature provides only limited information on the experiences of those involved in training, the narrative literature is reflective in tone and contains rich insights into the rewards and challenges of different approaches for both teachers and learners. It also includes several examples of innovative approaches to the learning and teaching of communication skills in social work education in the UK. For example, Rachman[78] describes a series of workshops on interviewing intended to promote student-centred learning. Students were actively involved in the planning, organisation and running of workshops that focused on their experiences in practice. Another imaginative response to the challenge of linking theory to practice is the use of large group role-play, as described by Moss[71]. This technique seeks to create a learning environment in which students can explore both structural and personal issues and dilemmas. In doing so it addresses the criticism that much interpersonal skills training is divorced from the critique of structural oppression that is central to social work education[54]. Koprowska[60] is concerned with the question of learning style and how to create a suitable learning environment for skill development. She provides an intriguing account of a workshop-based course on interview skills to demonstrate how Agazarian's theory of living human systems may be used to maximise opportunities for student learning.

4.2. Impact of training

What has been the impact, if any, of programmes for the learning of communication skills in social work education? Here, too, the evidence from the literature is often unclear. Overall, it would seem that behavioural approaches to communication skills training are helpful, when compared with formal classroom teaching alone or with opportunistic practice settings. They are generally well received by students, although reactions may vary among students with differing levels of practice experience[49]. However, there is also some evidence that behavioural approaches may have potentially negative effects, as in the finding by Barber[16] that training in specific micro-skills may increase student self-awareness, while reducing the student's client awareness. However, the findings from the literature should be treated with caution.

Despite efforts at systematic evaluation, methodological problems abound. As summarised by Dickson and Bamford[30], these include the use of single group post–test only designs[68], and the absence of random allocation to experimental and control groups[77].

There are indications in the literature that student learning persists beyond the end of training. A well-designed study by Nerdrum[73] found positive evidence that the effect of communication skills training is maintained over a follow–up period of 18 months. However, this study also indicated that the development of skilfulness was slow and dependent on specific training of therapeutic skills[72]. Evidence relating to the yet more important question of whether student learning is transferred into practice is much less encouraging. An investigation by Kopp and Butterfield[59] of student interview skills, before and after micro-skills training and subsequently with clients in practice settings, found an increased use of closed questions in the field, suggesting that student skills may have deteriorated in certain respects. Another much larger study by Collins and Bogo[24], investigating the transferability of laboratory-based learning of interview skills to encounters with service users, yielded similar findings. They looked at the communication of the basic skills of empathy, warmth and genuineness. They found a significant improvement in these skills when they tested students, through role-play interviews and a written test, before and after skills training. However, when the same students were assessed through tape-recordings of interviews with users, while on placement, the improvement was not sustained. The authors point to methodological issues, such as differences between the laboratory and field settings and in the measures used to assess skills in role-play and client interviews, which may explain the lack of skill transfer. Nevertheless they conclude that a more systematic competency-based approach to both the assessment and development of skills in the field would facilitate the transfer of laboratory-based learning. This message is supported by Dickson and Bamford[30] in their comprehensive review of the problem of skill transfer. The philosophy of 'train and hope' is, they argue, hopelessly inadequate. Instead attention should be paid to the content of training programmes to ensure relevance to the workplace, and to the student's personal attributes, such as personality and learning style. At the same time the role of the practice teacher in maximising college-based learning should be extended[138].

The definition and measurement of outcomes presents substantial difficulties for the evaluation of skills training programmes[25]. Typically, training outcomes are measured in terms of changes in the student rather than in service users[30]. Although studies such as Kopp and Butterfield[59] and Collins and Bogo[24] have attempted to assess changes in practice with service users, the outcome measures used relate to the quality of the student's communication with the service user, not the impact of that communication on the service user's behaviour or quality of life. A further criticism of many evaluative studies is that the effect of training is measured soon after it has ended and with no follow–up[30]. Another potential weakness in many studies is that the training and assessment of students depends on a single scale, such as Carkhuff's overall index of therapeutic communication, so that the effect of training is likely to be exaggerated[74].

The choices available to social work educators for the learning and teaching of communication skills have been further extended by the development of IT resources.

4.3. The contribution of IT and multi-media programs

The authors are acutely aware that the use of IT has now pervaded social work process and practice. It has also enriched much contemporary pedagogy, where there is a burgeoning literature now available (for an earlier landmark review, see Rafferty[79]). In social work practice, the electronic base of communication within and across professional boundaries has transformed practice skills. There are also current developments in online service provision that also raise important issues in communication skills. However, much of the literature that deals with these important developments falls outside the search terms for this particular review. This indicates the urgent need for a more comprehensive review of both narrative and evaluative studies of IT developments in the field of communication skills. Within the literature generated by the CRD search for this study, a key question concerned the contribution that such resources can make to the actual teaching of communication skills.

In the area of interpersonal skills training, the use of videotape and audiotape already has a long history, and the literature offers some evaluation of these 'practice skills aids'[78]. It is not surprising, however, that the IT revolution has seen a surge in the development of imaginative resources available to teacher and student alike.

Hansen et al[48], for example, assess the effectiveness of a multi-media communications skills training programme focusing on developing students' skills in 'paraphrasing' and ' perception checking', in order to enhance their professional listening skills. Engen and Dawson[39] evaluate an interactive CD Rom 'designed to provide realistic situations in which students can learn and evaluate their micro-counselling skills' in a program based in the University of Iowa. Resnick[80] explores ways in which a complex multi-media package involving graphics, text, video images and audio could be used to develop students' listening skills. Brawley[20] adopts a somewhat different approach in his article, where he describes how he teaches social work students to develop their advocacy skills through the mass media.

At this point it is helpful briefly to highlight some of the pedagogic assumptions underlying these developments. First, there is the assumption that the benefits from these often expensive and time-consuming developments will outweigh more traditional methods of teaching communication skills. Second, there is an uncritical assumption that 'experiential is best'. Third, the application of key underpinning knowledge, or a theoretical framework for such developments, is rarely articulated. Fourth, it is assumed that skilled tutors are needed to get the best out of students using such packages.

The literature frequently reflects the enthusiastic championing of IT-based approaches. Resnick[80], for example, proclaims that "The computer is infinitely patient, consistent, non-judgmental, and always supportive of students learning at their own pace and in their own place"[139]. The overall message drawn from the literature reviewed in this study, however, suggests that it is wise to be a little circumspect when looking at these developments from a UK perspective.

There are four main themes about these developments that have been identified.

First, the majority of the literature comes from the US and Canada, where Hansen et al[48] report an increase over a 20-year period (1977-97), from 1% to 70% in computer-based instruction. The strong 'learner-autonomy' ethos is cited as a major advantage in such programmes whereby the student can control the pace, timing and intensity of their learning. 'Interactivity' is seen to be an essential ingredient in helping students develop their skills. There is a general consensus in the literature reviewed that a majority of students placed some value on this style of learning.

Second, the transferability of such resources into a UK context is clearly an important issue when it comes to the fine-tuning of social work skills to specific contexts. This is an issue, of course, which also affects hard copy workbooks and textbooks such as Evans et al[40], Collins and Collins[26], and Cournoyer[28]. It is in the immediate and focused responses, in simulated as well as live contexts, that the quality of a student's skills is really enhanced.

Third, the IT packages currently available, including Procare's Interpersonal Skills CAL package[52], reviewed in Thompson[91] and MacFadden[63], all make the point that best practice will use such programmes to support, enhance and consolidate, not replace, face-to-face teaching.

Fourth, IT packages are expensive in time, money and developmental expertise, and often have a limited shelf life. Hansen et al[48], for example, report that their multi-media package took 30 people over two years to design and produce[140]. Careful decisions have to be made about whether the outcomes from such packages justify the initial – and updating – outlay costs.

In seeking to evaluate these developments, the strongest note of caution is issued by MacFadden et al[64]. They explore a set of issues and questions about how students are enabled to learn through such resources, and importantly, what the barriers are to learning through IT programs. These authors raise some crucially important issues when they discuss the 'human face of online education'. They argue that the literature which seeks to evaluate online learning rarely offers "any significant focus on the subjective experience of the most important partner in this new educational process – the learner"[141].

They make a significant contribution towards understanding the emotional impact of such programs on the learner and the facilitator. It is in both the student's and facilitator's interest that 'learning anxiety' is reduced, and that the program encourages early success for everyone involved[142]. It is often assumed that instructions given online will be easily understood and followed by students, whereas in fact it can be "extremely difficult to be totally clear and encompassing in explaining a task in written instruction"[143]. Facilitators have to grapple with issues like "getting lost in [cyber] space; what does 'bored' look like on-line? [and] how do theories of group dynamics apply to an on-line group?"[144].

Anyone involved in developing or seeking to make use of CAL would do well to explore the issues which MacFadden et al raise with thoughtful attention: unless they are dealt with properly, a successful outcome to a CAL program is likely to be very difficult to achieve.

4.4. Skills laboratories

Skills laboratories offer opportunities for simulated practice, with facilities for feedback often through video recording. With the likely development of skills laboratories with the new social work degree, it is instructive to review the literature to explore how some more familiar 'tried and tested' techniques have been evaluated. Mackey and Sheingold[65], for example, discuss the use of video laboratory work in Massachusetts to help clinical social work trainees to develop their empathy skills. Small groups of 4–5 trainees meet with a clinical instructor throughout the year, and each trainee is both interviewer and interviewee at least once in the group's programme. The interviews last 20 minutes, with an hour being given over to feedback, discussion and analysis. The creation of a safe learning environment where students can take risks, and where the tutor is able to facilitate a creative learning environment, is of paramount importance. It is 'out of the question' to let students simply 'go and play': the technique needs skilled and trained tutors who are able to use the equipment creatively and effectively. This view is confirmed by Vinton and Harrington[95] and by Pope[76], who describes the tutor's role as supporting and encouraging individual learning and small group work process[145]. By contrast, however, Rachman[78] reports that with video playback work, students felt more at ease and learned more when a tutor was not present.

In this context, an important caveat raised by Collins and Bogo[24] about the issue of transferability mentioned earlier in this study, deserves to be repeated:

> Mastery of skill in a laboratory does not necessarily mean that students will be able to utilize those skills ... with clients.[146]

They found that,

> ... a significant improvement in skill level for the students from the beginning of the laboratory to the end of the laboratory. However, students did not transfer their learned skills ... to the field....[147]

This finding, albeit some 20 years ago, raises a fundamental issue about all classroom-based communication skills work, and its transferability to practice. In the new social work degree, with its emphasis on service user and carer participation, it may be that this bridge will be more effectively crossed in future. Future evaluative work, however, will be essential.

4.5. Summary of narrative and evaluative concerns

The learning and teaching of communication skills in social work education in the UK has not been widely written up or evaluated. This is particularly the case with the multi-media approaches that are being developed in the UK. Instead, much of the evaluative literature is from North America and is concerned with the learning and teaching of interview skills. Although there is evidence that such training increases student skilfulness, it is often unclear whether these skills are maintained and transferred to work with service users. A general weakness in the evaluative literature is the lack of attention to outcomes in work with service users and to how these may be defined and measured.

The need to integrate communication skills training with practice learning is a recurrent theme. Innovative approaches that integrate the development of communication skills with other aspects of the social work curriculum, and seek to ensure an environment for learning, are now more in evidence in the UK literature. These require systematic evaluation to assess their effectiveness for future practice. Likewise, a comparison between an IT program approach and a more face-to-face experiential style, as encouraged by recent skills laboratory developments, would be particularly illuminating for the development of the new degree. We need to know not only what is the most effective use of resources, but also what prepares students best for the demands of their future social work careers. Finally, as indicated in the introduction to this chapter, there is a need for further work into evaluating the effectiveness of training in written communication skills.

5

Meeting particular communication needs

In this chapter attention is turned to the literature that addresses the learning and teaching of communication skills with service users with particular needs. The CRD search produced several articles that help students and practitioners to work with user groups with particular communication difficulties. Most of the articles are narrative accounts of short training courses in a range of settings and with a specific focus, for example, bereavement, challenging behaviour etc. Usually the formal input was described with examples of encounters between professionals and service users, which conveyed the central importance of communication in the delivery and experience of care services.

Learning disabilities have attracted some research interest. Dobson et al[34] describe a training programme which provides 'direct support skills' to adults with profound learning disabilities. Active participation of care staff with individual service users is video-recorded and assessed by the staff group. The learning of staff members is reinforced by observing their own interactions, the interventions of other staff members and the systematic feedback from the group. Boyle[19] describes the Sexual Attitude Reassessment Programme (SARS) used to explore and engender the skills needed to enable service users and care staff to discuss sexuality. This programme utilised films, lectures and small as well as large group discussions focused on sexuality and individuals with disability. Sutton and Thurman[89] focus on a training pack which provides factual information about 'challenging behaviour' and engages users through life story books, objects and pictures that signal intent.

Work with older adults has also been evidenced. Dreher[35] describes an earlier course that integrates knowledge of difficulties and strengths related to this life stage with a wide range of relevant communication skills and devices. Biographies of users are compiled by students and given to the user to provide new insights and perspectives on their lives and life experiences. Bender et al[17] describe a training course about the roles that women with dementia and other women of various ages have occupied during their lifetime. They outline the benefits that users and students obtained in the process of exploring the life roles of each participant. Benefits listed include being listened to, given space to talk, positive student learning and improved anti-discriminatory practice.

There were a number of articles that look at specific contexts. For example, Webster et al[96] use a multi-disciplinary approach and account for the organisational challenges that arise while developing a creative curriculum for working with substance misuse. The project involves academic and practice collaboration at a local level and emphasises the development of effective verbal and non-verbal communication and improved self-knowledge. Fieweger[41] describes a well-designed programme in a hospice setting. The article details the programme set up to support patients and family through the bereavement process. It describes different stages of awareness of impending death and the grief process. It also outlines the various skills and devices used by volunteers to engage the patient and the family. Mattern and Camp[67] present a case study of teaching care staff a few essential phrases in the foreign language employed by the service users with whom they work. They report slight increases in the interactions and reactions of carers and users over a three-month period of their programme.

The above needs may be seen as personal, but social workers also address particular needs that are more social. Brawley[20] adopts a wider view by showing how social workers can be trained in media advocacy with a view to correcting distorted messages about vulnerable people given by the press, developing policies and services and relaying important messages to large target audiences. Robinson[82] draws attention to the lack of information about inter-racial communication. She contends that research is 'eurocentric' in theory, method and focus. Her article is written in the UK and from a black perspective. She suggests guidelines for social work trainers dealing with inter-racial communication. Zapf[98] look at the dearth of recent literature in the US about cross-cultural practice. He explores the use of magic as a tool to explore uncertainty and promote cross-cultural practice.

Rosenfield explores what at first glance is a specialised skill of applying telephone technology to counselling. She has pioneered a great deal of the UK telephone 'hotline' industry. Her article argues for "the legitimisation of the telephone as a valid means by which to deliver counseling"[148], but also raises issues of 'net' meetings between counsellor and client, and text-phone work with deaf clients. More generally, however, there are implications for social work training where it is often simply assumed that students will be competent and skilful telephone users in their professional role. This is an important area where training could be developed in the skills laboratory context.

Generally the articles in this grouping produced examples of particular settings, specific user groups and specific techniques and provided good descriptions about the practical arrangements in terms of length and timing, content and follow-up arrangements. Many programmes involved small numbers of users and required significant resources of staff time. Staff used words, questions, symbols, pictures, life storybooks and so forth to develop and encourage the communication skills of users. Additionally they communicated with colleagues to check their learning and to ensure that the training programme was on track.

The lack of systematic evaluation was extremely disappointing. Many papers contained no evaluation. Those that included some evaluation[17] usually focused on the process, the benefits or products and mainly from the perspective of facilitators. There was a distinct lack of emphasis on systematic evaluation of data related to outcomes. Only two of the articles in this group[19,34] involved some degree of rigorous evaluation of outcomes. Recommendations were usually concerned with repeating, amending or expanding of the programmes. The views of service users were usually absent despite the emphasis on active participation and collaboration with service users. There was no real certainty about the user's awareness of the purpose of communication, and the meaning of the encounter was usually interpreted by professionals. There were no reports of measurement of skills prior to and at the end of the intervention. Where there was reported evidence of an increase in staff skills, no evidence was produced about the sustainability or transference of these skills to other situations. The articles from education settings provided information on theory and suggested content for training programmes, but they did not report on actual programmes and no attention was given to student characteristics and potential.

The absence of a coherent body of literature is itself interesting. It could be due to the fact that pedagogic research is not highly valued in Research Exercise Assessment (RAE) rating and, therefore, there is less incentive for academics to work in this area. Or it may be due to the fact that research funding for a substantive piece of pedagogic research is difficult to acquire. However, it is important to note that the Economic and Social Research Council (ESRC) has recently made funding available for pedagogic research. This must be welcomed if it leads to rigorous research and to a greater focus on helping students to learn how to work with user groups with particular communication difficulties.

6

Summary of key findings

The overarching finding, common to all aspects of this review, was the absence of a coherent body of literature which provided a clear framework for the design of programmes seeking to teach communication skills to social work students. Consequently, the following sub-sections focus primarily on the current gaps in this area of social work education. Having acknowledged that this is the current situation, there were some exceptionally thoughtful and thought-provoking articles. These have proved influential in the compiling of this review. These examples are listed in the annotated bibliography (**Appendix B**).

6.1. Theoretical underpinnings

As has been acknowledged, few of the articles made explicit the theoretical underpinning knowledge on which their work was based, and it appears that a lot of work in communication skills is undertaken without a firm theoretical foundation. This suggests that this subject tends to be taught in a 'hands-on' experiential way without an accompanying academic rigour. This may also be reflected in the number of narrative articles in the review. These describe innovative ways of working, but tend to lack a critical evaluative dimension. It is clear that these concerns need to be researched in order to ensure that the learning and teaching of communication skills is theoretically informed, and critically evaluated for their relevance to communication in social work practice.

6.2. The context and style of learning and teaching

The diverse range of approaches to the teaching of communication skills generates a number of challenging questions. First, how can educators (in academic and in practice settings) be effectively resourced to undertake this teaching task? To teach communication skills effectively educators need to possess the very skills they are teaching. It remains unclear, however, where and how educators are trained both in the content of teaching communication skills and in the specific approach being adopted. This latter aspect of the teaching task is particularly pertinent in light of the growing interest in technologically orientated programme designs.

Second, what do students require in order for their learning to be maximised? Within the literature reviewed there was surprisingly little mention of theories and models of adult learning. Few of the studies reviewed suggested a conceptual framework within which a range of different learning styles could be accommodated. This gap in the literature is even more surprising given government documents urging teachers to increase the range of learning modes offered, and requires further attention.

6.3. The transferability and sustainability of learning and teaching

A recurrent theme arising from the literature was the concern about the transferability of learning from the academy to practice. The current picture is of a marked lack of consistency and continuity between the academic and practice settings. The nature of the learning appears to require professional and organisational support in both contexts, yet the organisational needs involved in learning and teaching communication skills were not raised by many of the studies reviewed. If this gap is not addressed, it is likely to continue to have a negative impact on the ability of students and practitioners to acquire and perfect specific skills. How to ensure the transferability of skills, so that these are reliable and enduring across different, often difficult, situations, remains an under-researched area. This question is made more difficult because social work lacks a common language from which to describe and conceptualise key issues relating to learning and teaching of social work skills.

6.4. Evaluation

The review highlighted a dearth of writing that addressed the challenging issues of evaluating the learning and teaching of communication skills. This situation has serious implications for the issues of transferability, referred to above, as without robust evaluative strategies and studies the risks of fragmented and context-restricted learning are heightened. More work is needed on various methodological aspects of evaluation – particularly on the definition and measurement of outcomes, and the ways technological aids, developed through various IT resources, are employed in supporting face-to-face learning and teaching.

6.5. User involvement

User involvement in the teaching process was notably absent. Given the relatively recent emergence of interest in this area it is not surprising this is the case. The picture is not entirely bleak, however, as the findings of the Brunel Practice Survey indicate that there may be more initiatives in operation which involve service users than have yet been reported in the literature[33]. The centrality of user views and involvement in the design and delivery of the new degree makes it imperative that educators begin to develop partnerships in this area of learning and teaching. This would enable educators to utilise the insights and skills that these individuals bring to the educational process within social work.

6.6. Transcultural communication and communication with people with particular needs

The literature review identified very little with regard to transcultural communication skills in relation to people with particular needs, which underlines the importance of further work being done in this specific area. However, an important text in this field is the work of Robinson[81] who looks at inter-ethnic communication skills in relation to current social work and healthcare literature on this theme. In addition to people from minority ethnic groups, this issue is also important for other service users and social work students. For example, some people have Welsh as their first language. In this context, it is important to remember that language is more than a mode of communication. It is one of the major ways that we develop our unique and distinctive identity as human beings. One of the policy aims of the Higher Education Funding Council for Wales (HEFCW) is to ensure that the English and Welsh languages are treated equally, so that Welsh-speaking social work students and service users are not disadvantaged. Under the CCWs' *Rules for the approval of courses in social work*, programmes are required to have systems to audit and evaluate their provision for students who wish to learn and be assessed through the medium of Welsh.

The review considered only a small number of studies that focused on learning and teaching communication skills related to meeting particular communication needs. Clearly, because the brief of social work is so wide, service users are likely to present a wide range of particular needs. The challenge for social work practitioners is to clearly define these needs and then properly address them. The breadth of practice necessitates practitioners and service users contributing to the teaching process in order to ensure that the specific needs of service users groups are accurately conveyed and understood.

The preceding discussion is summarised in the next chapter in the form of key messages. These provide readers of the knowledge review with easy access to the pertinent issues arising from this review.

7

Key messages

The theoretical underpinning in relation to the learning and teaching of communication skills is underdeveloped. For example, there is little coherence in the literature to assist educators to teach effectively, and little coverage of students' different learning styles. These differences are reflected in the divergent range of models identified by the Brunel Practice Survey[33] and also in research undertaken by Marsh and Triseliotis[66].

In light of the requirements of the new degree in relation to the learning and teaching of communication skills, several aspects require particular attention:

- there is an absence of literature that addresses service user involvement in, and perspectives on, the learning and teaching of communication skills;
- greater focus is needed on the importance of transcultural communication skills given the limited literature and research in this area;
- encouragement needs to be given to enable practitioners to contribute to teaching/learning in all aspects of practice, particularly those areas such as transcultural communication skills, where there is a serious lack of literature and research;
- there is scope for more work to be done on the learning and teaching of specific communication skills associated with specific theoretical approaches;
- the lack of a 'common language' means that greater rigour is needed when using such terms as *generalist, specialist* and *advanced practice skills, micro-skills and macro-skills; interventions,* and so on;
- the processes involved in teaching communication skills require as much attention as the content of the teaching;
- evaluative studies which focus on the learning and teaching of interviewing and listening skills suggest that the improvements made in simulated settings do not automatically transfer to practice settings

with service users. The integration of communication skills training with practice learning is seen as crucial here;

- the increasing use of computer-based programs and skills laboratories is described in the literature, but the limited evaluation of such resources suggests that they are best used to support face-to-face teaching rather than as 'stand-alone' training in communication skills;
- the relative paucity of evaluative literature indicates that there is an urgent need to develop a robust methodology, particularly with regard to defining and measuring the effectiveness of communication skills with service users.

8

Conclusion and challenges
for the future

In light of the requirements of the new degree, the learning of communication skills needs to be seen as a priority in social work education. Although this knowledge review has not been able to identify from the literature reviewed a unified body of knowledge on which such teaching programmes can be based, it has highlighted those aspects that need further attention.

First, the practical constraints on this project made it impossible for the authors to address three significant aspects of the literature generated by the CRD search:

- the literature on learning and teaching of communication skills in other sectors such as medicine, nursing and allied health professionals;
- the literature on improving communications skills of users;
- the learning and teaching of communication skills in relation to working interprofessionally.

It is anticipated that further work will be commissioned by SCIE to examine these issues.

Second, it is recognised that there is far greater expertise in existence than is reflected in the literature. The findings of the Brunel Practice Survey[33] indicate that there is a considerable amount of innovative practice being undertaken in this field that is, as yet, barely covered in the literature. It is hoped, therefore, that this knowledge review can serve as a catalyst to educators in two ways: by encouraging educators to write for publication their knowledge and experience on this aspect of education, and to address the gaps in existing knowledge by undertaking research in the areas identified in the review's key messages.

Third, the theoretical knowledge base that underpins the learning and teaching of communication skills needs to be made more explicit, adopting the same academic rigour used in other areas of social work research and practice theory. The review was enriched by the international scope of the articles provided by the search, but the transferability of much of the material to the UK context is far from straightforward. Furthermore, more research is needed on the transferability of communication skills learning and teaching from the university to practice contexts, and across different settings and service user groups.

Finally, there is an urgent need to undertake a comprehensive and critical review of the contribution that IT is making to the development of communication skills within social work process, practice and pedagogy.

If these challenges can be met, there is the potential for the learning and teaching of communication skills in social work to be built on firm foundations – an essential prerequisite for effective teaching, learning and practice.

References

1   Cross, C.P. (ed) (1974) *Interviewing and communication in social work*, London: Routledge and Kegan Paul.

2   Day, P.D. (1972) *Communication in social work*, Oxford: Permagon Press.

3   Mayer, J.E. and Timms, N. (1970) *The client speaks*, London: Routledge.

4   Nelson, J.C. (1980) *Communication theory and social work practice*, New Jersey: Prentice-Hall.

5   Coulshed, V. and Orme, J. (1998). *Social work practice: An introduction*, Basingstoke: Macmillan/British Association of Social Workers, p 2.

6   Arnold, E. and Sedley, S. (1987) *Whose child? The report of the public inquiry into the death of Tyra Henry*, London: Lambeth.

7   Blom Cooper, L. (1987) *A child in the mind: The report of the commission of inquiry into the circumstances surrounding the death of Kimberley Carlile*, London: Greenwich.

8   Gough, D. (1993) *Child abuse interventions: A review of the research literature*, London: HMSO.

9   Laming, H. (2003) *The Victoria Climbié inquiry: Report of an inquiry*, London: The Stationery Office.

10   Topss (Training Organisation for the Personal Social Services) (2002) *The national occupational standards for social work*, Working copy, May.

11   QAA (Quality Assurance Agency) for Higher Education (2000) *Subject benchmark statement: Social policy and administration and social work. Quality Assurance Agency for Higher Education: An introduction*, QAA for Higher Education (www.qaa.ac.uk/crntwork/benchmark/socialwork.pdf).

12   DH (Department of Health) (2002) *Requirements for social work training*, London: DH.

13   DH (2002) op cit, pp 3-4.

14   Pierson, J. and Thomas, M. (2000) *Collins dictionary of social work*, London, Collins, p 95.

15   Allan, K. (2001) *Communication and consultation: Exploring ways for staff to involve people with dementia developing services*, Bristol/York: The Policy Press/ Joseph Rowntree Foundation.

16   Barber, J. (1988) 'Are microskills worth teaching?', *Journal of Social Work Education*, vol 24, no 1, pp 3-12.

17   Bender, M., Horton, V. and Rees, F. (2000) 'Where women meet: aren't we more alike than different?', *Journal of Dementia Care*, vol 8, no 6, pp 20-2.

18 Bondareva, L.V., Kovaleva, Z.I. and Lebedev, V.B. (1998) 'Contemporary foundations of sociopsychological training of social workers', *Journal of Russian and East European Psychology*, vol 36, no 3, pp 92-6.

19 Boyle, P.S. (1993) 'Training in sexuality and disability: preparing social workers to provide services to individuals with disabilities', *Journal of Social Work and Human Sexuality*, vol 8, no 2, pp 45-62.

20 Brawley, E.A. (1997) 'Teaching social work students to use advocacy skills through the mass media', *Journal of Social Work Education*, vol 33, no 3, pp 445-60.

21 Bricker-Jenkins, M. (1990) 'Another approach to practice and training', *Public Welfare*, vol 48, no 2, pp 11-16.

22 Burnard, P. (1989) *Counselling skills for health professionals*, London: Chapman and Hall/CRC.

23 Cohen, J. and Cohen, B.Z. (1998) 'Graduating social work students' communication competencies and motivations: their effects on satisfaction with social work', *International Social Work*, vol 41, no 3, pp 357-70.

24 Collins, D. and Bogo, M. (1986) 'Competency-based field instruction: bridging the gap between laboratory and field learning', *Clinical Supervisor*, vol 4, no 3, pp 39-52.

25 Collins, D., Gabor, P. and Ing, C. (1987) 'Communication skill training in child care: the effects of preservice and inservice training', *Child and Youth Care Quarterly*, vol 16, pp 106-15.

26 Collins, J. and Collins, M. (1992) *Social skills training and the professional helper*, Chichester, NY: Wiley.

27 Corcoran, K.J. (1982) 'Behavioral and nonbehavioral methods of developing two types of empathy: a comparative study', *Journal of Education for Social Work*, vol 18, no 3, pp 85-93.

28 Cournoyer, B. (2000) *The social work skills workbook* (3rd edn), Belmont, CA: Brooks/Cole Publishing Co.

29 Dickson, D. (1997) *Communication skills training for health professionals*, London: Chapman and Hall.

30 Dickson, D. and Bamford, D. (1995) 'Improving the interpersonal skills of social-work students – the problem of transfer of training and what to do about it', *British Journal of Social Work*, vol 25, no 1, pp 85-105.

31 Dickson, D. and Mullan, T. (1990) 'An empirical investigation of the effects of a microcounselling programme with social work students: the acquisition and transfer of component skills', *Counselling Psychology Quarterly*, vol 3, no 3, pp 267-83.

[32] Dillard, J.M. and Reilly, R.R. (eds) (1988) *Systematic interviewing: Communication skills for professional effectiveness*, Columbus, OH: Merrill Publishing Co.

[33] Dinham, A., Aymer, C., Okitikpi, C., Googyer, T. and Randall, B. (2003) 'Learning and teaching in social work: communication – a practice survey', unpublished, London: SCIE.

[34] Dobson, S., Upadhyaya, S. and Stanley, B. (2002) 'Using an interdisciplinary approach to training to develop the quality of communication with adults with profound learning disabilities by care staff', *International Journal of Language & Communication Disorders*, vol 37, no 1, pp 41-57.

[35] Dreher, B.-B. (1983) 'Communicating with the elderly: a new service course?', *Communication-Education*, vol 32, no 4, pp 421-4.

[36] Edwards, J.B. and Richards, A. (2002) 'Relational teaching: a view of relational teaching in social work education', *Journal of Teaching in Social Work*, vol 22, no 1/2, pp 33-48.

[37] Egan, G. (2002) *The skilled helper: A systematic approach to effective helping*, Pacific Grove, CA: Brooks/Cole.

[38] Egan, G. and McGourty, R. (eds) (2002) *Exercises in helping skills: A training manual to accompany 'The skilled helper'*, Pacific Grove, CA: Brooks /Cole.

[39] Engen, H.B. and Dawson, R.D. (2002) 'Counseling simulations: an interactive CD-ROM approach', *Journal of Technology in Human Services*, vol 20, no 3/4, pp 301-16.

[40] Evans, D.R., Hearn, M.T., Uhlemann, M.R. and Ivey, A.E. (1989) *Essential interviewing: A programmed approach to effective communication*. Belmont, CA: Brooks/Cole Publishing Co.

[41] Fieweger, M.A. (1987) 'Interpersonal communication instruction in the non-traditional context: teaching communication strategies in a hospice setting', Paper presented at the Annual Meeting of the Western Speech Communication Association (58th, Salt Lake City, UT), 14-17 February.

[42] Fischer, J. (1975) 'Training for effective therapeutic practice', *Psychotherapy: Theory, research and practice*, vol 12, pp 118-23.

[43] Fischer, J. (1978) *Effective casework practice: An eclectic approach*, New York, NY: McGraw Hill.

[44] Freire, P. (1972) *Pedagogy of the oppressed*, Harmondsworth: Penguin.

[45] Freire, P. and Shor, I. (1987) *Pedagogy for liberation: Dialogues on transforming education*, Basingstoke: Macmillan.

[46] Gordon, T. and Edwards, W.S. (1995) *Making the patient your partner: Communication skills for doctors and other caregivers*, Westport, CT: Auburn House/Greenwood Publishing Group, Inc.

47 Hansen, E.J. (1994) 'Interactive video for reflection: learning theory and a new use of the medium', *Computers in Human Services*, vol 11, no 1/2, pp 31-47.

48 Hansen, F.C., Resnick, H. and Galea, J. (2002) 'Better listening: paraphrasing and perception checking – a study of the effectiveness of a multimedia skills training program', *Journal of Technology in Human Services*, vol 20, no 3/4, pp 317-31.

49 Hargie, O. and Bamford, D. (1984) 'A comparison of the reactions of pre-service and in-service social workers to microtraining', *Vocational-Aspect-of-Education*, vol 36, no 95, pp 87-91.

50 Hargie, O.D.W. (ed) (1997) *The handbook of communication skills*, London: Routledge.

51 Hargie, O., Saunders, C. and Dickson, D. (2002) *Social skills in interpersonal communication*, London: Routledge.

52 Hopkins, T., Rafferty, J., Glastonbury, J. and Columbi, D. (1996) *Interpersonal skills for social work, Procare*, Centre for Human Service Technology, University of Southampton (www.chst.soton.ac.uk/procare/).

53 Jackson, E. (1987) 'Specificity and generality of internal empathy in facilitative behavior and communicated empathy: a path-analytic study', *Social Work Research and Abstracts*, vol 23, no 3, pp 4-9.

54 Jessup, H. and Rogerson, S. (1999) 'Postmodernism and the teaching and practice of interpersonal skills', in J. Pease and J. Fook, *Social work practice: Postmodern critical perspectives*, London: Routledge.

55 Jordan, J.V., Kaplan, A.G., Miller, J.B., Stiver, I.P. and Surrey, J.L. (eds) (1991) *Women's growth and connection: Writings from the stone center*, New York, NY: Guilford Press.

56 Kadushin, A. and Kadushin, G. (1997) *The social work interview*, New York, NY: Columbia University Press.

57 Keefe, T. (1979) 'The development of empathic skill: a study', *Journal of Education for Social Work*, vol 15, no 2, pp 30-7.

58 Kolb, D.A. (1984) *Experiential learning: Experience as the source of learning and development*, London: Prentice Hall.

59 Kopp, J. and Butterfield, W. (1985) 'Changes in graduate students' use of interviewing skills from the classroom to the field', *Journal of Social Service Research*, vol 9, no 1, pp 65-88.

60 Koprowska, J. (2003) 'The right kind of telling? Locating the teaching of interview skills with a systems framework', *British Journal of Social Work*, vol 33, pp 291-308.

[61] Kornbeck, J. (2001) '"Gemeinschaft" skills versus "Gesellschaft" skills in social work education and practice. Applying Tönnies' dichotomy for a model of intercultural communication', *Social Work Education*, vol 20, no 2, pp 247-61.

[62] Lishman, J. (1994) *Communication in social work*, Basingstoke: Macmillan.

[63] MacFadden, R.J. (1999) 'Interpersonal skills – social work', *Journal of Technology in Human Services*, vol 16, no 1, pp 71-5.

[64] MacFadden, R.J., Maiter, S. and Dumbrill, G.C. (2002) 'High tech and high touch: the human face of online education', *Journal of Technology in Human Services*, vol 20, no 3/4, pp 283-300.

[65] Mackey, R.A. and Sheingold, A. (1990) 'Thinking empathically: the video laboratory as an integrative resource', *Source Clinical Social Work Journal*, vol 18, pp 423-32.

[66] Marsh, P. and Triseliotis, J. (1996) *Ready to practice? Social workers and probation officers: Their training and first year at work*, Aldershot: Avebury.

[67] Mattern, J.M. and Camp, C.J. (1998) 'Increasing the use of foreign language phrases by direct care staff in a nursing home setting', *Clinical Gerontologist*, vol 19, no 3, pp 84-6.

[68] Mayo, M.H. (1979) 'Teaching communication/interviewing skills to urban undergraduate social work students', *Journal of Education for Social Work*, vol 15, no 1, pp 66-71.

[69] McMahon, L. (1995) 'Developing skills in therapeutic communication in daily living with emotionally disturbed children and young people', *Journal of Social Work Practice*, vol 9, no 2, pp 199-214.

[70] Morton, T.D. and Lindsey, E.W. (1987) 'Toward a model for interpersonal helping skills use and training in public welfare practice', *Journal of Continuing Social Work Education*, vol 4, no 1, pp 18-24.

[71] Moss, B. (2000) 'The use of large-group role-play techniques in social work education', *Social Work Education*, vol 19, no 53, pp 471-83.

[72] Nerdrum, P. (1996) 'Steps towards an integration of basic therapeutic skills – a qualitative study of the development of the ideas of 15 social-work students about being helpful to clients', *Scandinavian Journal of Social Welfare*, vol 5, no 3, pp 175-84.

[73] Nerdrum, P. (1997) 'Maintenance of the effect of training in communication skills: a controlled follow-up study of level of communicated empathy', *British Journal of Social Work*, vol 27, no 5, pp 705-22.

[74] Nerdrum, P. and Lundquist, K. (1995) 'Does participation in communication skills training increase student levels of communicated empathy? A controlled outcome study', *Journal of Teaching in Social Work*, vol 12, no 1/2, pp 139-57.

[75] Nunnally, E. and Moy, C. (1989) *Communication basics for human service professionals*, Thousand Oaks, CA: Sage Publications, Inc.

[76] Pope, P. (2002) 'Enhancing the development of effective one-to-one skills for practice', *Practice*, vol 14, no 3, pp 51-8.

[77] Pymn, B. and Marsh, P. (1984) 'The development of socially skilled practice: social skills training in social work education', *British Journal of Social* Work, vol 14, pp 337-45.

[78] Rachman, R. (1987) 'Student centred learning', *Practice*, vol 1, no 2, pp 173-89.

[79] Rafferty, J. (1998) 'Changing to learn: learning to change', *Computers in Human Services*, vol 15, no 2/3, pp 159-69.

[80] Resnick, H. (1998) 'Paraphrase★II: a listening skills training program for human service students', *Computers in Human Services*, vol 15, no 2/3, pp 89-96.

[81] Robinson, L. (1998) *Race: Communication and the caring professions*, Buckingham: Open University Press.

[82] Robinson, L. (1995) 'Interracial communication and social work practice: some issues and guidelines for social work trainers and practitioners', *Journal of Practice and Staff Development*, vol 4, no 4, pp 34-44.

[83] Rogers, C.R. (1951) *Client-centred therapy*, Boston, MA: Houghton Mifflin.

[84] Rogers, C.R. (1961) *On becoming a person*, Boston, MA: Houghton Mifflin.

[85] Rosenfield, M. (2002) 'Electronic technology for social work education and practice: the application of telephone technology to counseling', *Journal of Technology in Human Services*, vol 20, no 1/2, pp 173-81.

[86] Schön, D. (1983) *The reflective practitioner: How professionals think in action*, London: Temple Smith.

[87] Schön, D. (1987) *Educating the reflective practitioner*, London: Jossey-Bass.

[88] Seden, J. (1999) *Counselling skills in social work practice*, Buckingham: Open University Press.

[89] Sutton, K. and Thurman, S. (1998) 'Challenging communication: people with learning disabilities who challenge services', *International Journal of Language & Communication Disorders*, vol 33, Supplement, pp 415-20.

[90] Taylor, Z. (1999) 'Values, theories and methods in social work education', *International Social Work*, vol 42, no 3, pp 309-18.

91   Thompson, N. (1997) 'Interpersonal skills–social work module', *New Technology in the Human Services*, vol 10, no 2, pp 21-2.

92   Thompson, N. (2002) *People skills: A guide to effective practice in the human services*, Basingstoke: Macmillan Palgrave.

93   Toseland, R. and Spielberg, G. (1982) 'The development of helping skills in undergraduate social work education: model and evaluation', *Journal of Education for Social Work*, vol 18, no 1, pp 66-73.

94   Trevithick, P. (2000) *Social work skills: A practice handbook*, Buckingham: Open University Press.

95   Vinton, L. and Harrington, P. (1994) 'An evaluation of the use of videotape in teaching empathy', *Journal of Teaching in Social Work*, vol 9, no 1/2, pp 71-84.

96   Webster, B.J., Yardley, J., Hegan, L. and Tebano, C. (2002) 'Developing a creative curriculum for those working with clients who misuse substances', *The Drug and Alcohol Professional*, vol 2, no 1, pp 29-35.

97   Worsley, J. (1989) *Taking good care: A handbook for care assistants*, Mitcham: Age Concern England.

98   Zapf, M.K. (1989) 'Puzzles and power: magic as a classroom resource for social work educators', *Canadian Social Work Review/Revue canadienne de service social*, vol 6, no 2, pp 153-62.

99   Hopkins, G. (1998) *Plain English for social services: A guide for better communication*, Lyme Regis: Russell House.

100   Hopkins, G. (1998) *The write stuff: A guide to effective writing in social care and related services*, Lyme Regis: Russell House.

101   O'Hagan, K. (1996) *Competence in social work practice: A practical guide for professionals*, London: Jessica Kingsley Publishers.

102   Prince, K. (1996) *Boring records? Communication, Speech and writing in social work*, London: Jessica Kingsley.

103   Rawlins, K. (1993) *Presentation and communication skills: A handbook for practitioners*, London: Macmillan.

104   Robinson, M. (2002) *Communication and health in a multi-ethnic society*, Bristol: The Policy Press.

105   Thompson, N. (2003) *Communication and language. A handbook of theory an practice*, Basingstoke: Palgrave, Macmillan.

106   Dickson, D. and Bamford, D. (1995) op cit, p 85.

107   Marsh, P. and Treseliotis, J. (1996) op cit, p 51.

108   Marsh, P. and Treseliotis, J. (1996) op cit, p 52.

109   Koprowska, J. (2003) op cit, p 291.

110   Taylor, Z. (1999) op cit, p 316.

[111] Jessup, H. and Rogerson, S. (1999) op cit, p 162.

[112] Hepworth, D.H. and Larsden, J.A. (1990) *Direct social work practice*, Belmont, CA: Wadsworth.

[113] Corcoran, K.J. (1982) op cit, p 86.

[114] Cohen, J. and Cohen, B.Z. (1998) op cit, p 358.

[116] Schön, D. (1987) op cit, p 17.

[117] Miller, J.B. and Stiver, J. (1997) *The healing connection*, Boston, MA: Beacon Press.

[118] Edwards, J.B. and Richards, A. (2002) op cit, p 43.

[119] Foucault, M. (1979) *Discipline and punish: The birth of the prison*, Harmondsworth: Penguin.

[120] Jessup, H. and Rogerson, S. (1999) op cit, p 177.

[121] Koprowska, J. (2003) op cit, p 296.

[122] Koprowska, J. (2003) op cit, p 306.

[123] Dreyfus, H. and Dreyfus, S. (1986) *Mind over machine: The power of human intuition and expertise in an era of the computer*, New York, NY: The Free Press.

[124] Hansen, E.J. (1994) op cit, p 31.

[125] Winnicott, D.W. (1958) *Through paediatrics to psycho-analysis*, London: Hogarth.

[126] Winnicott, D.W. (1965) *The maturational process and the facilitating environment: Studies in the theory of emotional development*, London: Hogarth Press.

[127] Winnicott, D.W. (1971) *Playing and reality*, London: Tavistock.

[128] Dockar-Drysdale, B. (1990) *The provision of primary experience: Winnicotian work with children*, London: Free Association Books.

[129] Bricker-Jenkins, M. (1990) op cit, p 11.

[130] NAW (National Assembly for Wales) (2003) *Requirements for an award of a degree in social work*, Cardiff: NAW.

[131] Dinham, A. et al (2003) op cit, p 5.

[132] Dickson, D. and Bamford, D. (1995) op cit, p 98.

[133] Coulshed, V. and Orme, J. (1998) *Social work practice: An introduction*, Basingstoke: Macmillan/British Association of Social Workers.

[134] Marsh, P. and Treseliotis, J. (1996) op cit, p 205.

[135] Toseland, R. and Spielberg, G. (1982) op cit, pp 66-7.

[136] Nerdrum, P. and Lundquist, K. (1995) op cit, p 145.

[137] Dickson, D. and Mullan, T. (1990) op cit, p 272.

[138] Dickson, D. and Bamford, D. (1995) op cit, p 102.

[139] Resnick, H. (1998) op cit, p 90.

[140] Hansen, F.C. et al (2002) op cit, p 319.

141 MacFadden, R.J. et al (2002) op cit, p 284.

142 MacFadden, R.J. et al (2002) op cit, p 286.

143 MacFadden, R.J. et al (2002) op cit, p 291.

144 MacFadden, R.J. et al (2002) op cit, p 293.

145 Pope, P. (2002) op cit, p 57.

146 Collins, D. and Bogo, M. (1986) op cit, p 39.

147 Collins, D. and Bogo, M. (1986) op cit, p 42.

148 Rosenfield, M. (2002) op cit, p 174.

149 Egan, G. (1990) *The skilled helper: A systematic approach to effective helping*, Pacific Grove, CA: Brooks/Cole.

150 Barber, G., Goldberg, G., Savage, R. and Fisher, S. (1983) 'A comparison of knowledge and attitude change using teleconferencing and programmed instruction', *Journal of Continuing Social Work Education*, vol 2, no 2, pp 36-9.

151 Carrillo, D. and Thyer, B.A. (1994) 'Advanced standing and two-year program MSW students: an empirical investigation of foundation interviewing skills', *Journal of Social Work Education*, vol 30, no 3, pp 377-87.

152 Cetingok, M. (1988) 'Simulation group exercises and development of interpersonal skills: social work administration students' assessment in a simple time-series design framework', *Small Group Behavior*, vol 19, pp 395-404.

153 Corcoran, K.J. (1983) 'Emotional separation and empathy', *Journal of Clinical Psychology*, vol 39, no 5, pp 667-71.

154 Finn, J. (1990) 'Teaching computer telecommunications to social work undergraduates', *Arete*, vol 15, no 2, pp 38-43.

155 Gelfand, B. (1990) 'The reflective log, an essential teaching instrument in assisting students to integrate theory with practice in a communication skills laboratory', *Canadian Social Work Review/Revue canadienne de service social*, vol 7, no 2, pp 273-82.

156 Kurtz, G. and Dickinson, N.S. (1981) 'Assertive skills for social service workers', *Journal of Continuing Social Work Education*, vol 1, no 4, pp 7-10.

157 Lindsey, E.W., Yarbrough, D.B. and Morton, T.D. (1987) 'Evaluating interpersonal skills training for public welfare staff', *Social Service Review*, vol 61, no 4, pp 623-35.

158 Loewenstein, S.F. (1985) 'Group theory in an experimental group', *Social Work with Groups*, vol 8, no 1, pp 25-40.

159 Lordan, N. (1996) 'The use of sculpt in social groupwork education', *Groupwork*, vol 9, no 1, pp 62-79.

160 Minor, N.K.M. and McGauley, L. (1988) 'A different approach: dialogue in education', *Journal of Teaching in Social Work*, vol 2, no 1, pp 127-40.

161 Winnicott, C. (1996) 'Communicating with children', *Smith College Studies in Social Work*, vol 66, no 2, pp 117-28.

162 Alagaratnam, W.J. (1982) 'Rethinking interpersonal communication research. Methodological problems in design and evaluation and suggestions for a multimodal approach to social skills training', Proceedings of the 23rd annual conference of the Royal College of Nursing Research Society, University of Durham, Royal College of Nursing.

163 Arkansas State Dept (1992) Arkansas long-term care facility nursing assistant training curriculum, Little Rock, Arkansas State Department of Human Services.

164 Bal, A., Britnell, J., McCarthy, C. and Samuels, S. (1995) 'Evaluation of an interactive multimedia application to learn interpersonal skills', *Medinfo*, vol 8, no 2, p 1694.

165 Berkman, B. and Rutchick, I. (1987) 'Improving the sensitivity of health professionals to the needs of patients and families: an experiment', *Small Group Behavior*, vol 18, pp 239-53.

166 Bookhagen, A.D., Egenast, D.P. and McGowan, R.J. (2002) 'Multimedia interactive training development-journey: discovering social services CD-ROM', *Journal of Technology in Human Services*, vol 20, no 3/4, pp 333-44.

167 Bowman, R.P. and Myrick, R.D. (1985) 'Students as peer helpers: an untapped resource', *Social Work in Education*, vol 7, no 2, pp 124-33.

168 Brownstein, C. and McGill, S. (1984) 'Practice workshops: a model for teaching base social work practice', *Arete*, vol 9, no 1, pp 48-53.

169 Burton, M.V. (1991) 'Counselling in routine care: a client-centred approach', in M. Watson, *Cancer patient care: Psychosocial treatment methods*, Leicester: BPS Books, pp 74-93.

170 Campbell, R.V. (1989) 'Teaching counseling and problem-solving skills to professionals working with child abuse and neglect families', *Dissertation Abstracts International, A: The Humanities and Social Sciences*, vol 49, pp 1962-A.

171 Carpenter, M.C. (1997) *Effects of interpersonal skills training on nurse aides' client care*, Texas: Texas Woman's University, p 160.

172 Cauble, A.E. and Dinkel, J.L. (2002) 'The development of a multimedia training project: rewards and challenges of the multidisciplinary team', *Journal of Technology in Human Services*, vol 20, no 3/4, pp 345-68.

173 Coleman, W.L. and Lindsay, R.L. (1998) 'Making friends: helping children develop interpersonal skills', *Contemporary Pediatrics*, vol 15, no 8, pp 111-12.

174 Collins, D.G. (1985) 'A study of transfer of interviewing skills from the laboratory to the field', *Dissertation Abstracts*, vol 21, no 3, p 1028.

175 Costello, S. (1995) 'Practice forum: training in advanced family casework for social workers', *Australian Social Work*, vol 48, no 4, pp 29-40.

176 Donaldson, D. (1999) 'Effective ways to communicate with the dying', *Caring*, vol 18, no 2, p 18.

177 Done, D.J. and Thomas, J.A. (2001) 'Training in communication skills for informal carers of people suffering from dementia: a cluster randomized clinical trial comparing a therapist led workshop and booklet', *International Journal of Geriatric Psychiatry*, vol 16, no 8, pp 816-21.

178 Dyche, L. and Zayas, L.H. (2001) 'Cross-cultural empathy and training the contemporary psychotherapist', *Clinical Social Work Journal*, vol 29, no 3, pp 245-58.

179 Engram, B.E. (1981) 'Communication skills training for rehabilitation counselors working with older persons', *Journal of Rehabilitation*, October-December.

180 Erera, P.I. (1997) 'Empathy training for helping professionals: model and evaluation', *Journal of Social Work Education*, vol 33, no 2, pp 245-60.

181 Everson, J.M. (1995) *Transition services for youths who are deaf-blind: a 'best practices' guide for educators*, Sands Point, NY: Helen Keller National Center, Technical Assistance Center.

182 Faulkner, A., Argent, J. and Jones, A. (2001) 'Effective communication in health care: exploring the skills of the teachers', *Patient Education and Counseling*, vol 45, no 3, pp 227-32.

183 Feil, N. (1993) *The Validation breakthrough: Simple techniques for communicating with people with 'Alzheimer's-type dementia'*, Baltimore, MD: Health Professions Press.

184 Feldt, K.S. and Ryden, M.B. (1992) 'Aggressive behavior. Educating nursing assistants', *Journal of Gerontological Nursing*, vol 18, no 5, pp 3-12.

185 Fitz Ritson, S.H. (1997) 'The effectiveness of social problem-solving training versus Egan consultation skills training for new casemanagers', *Dissertation Abstracts International: Section B*, vol 57, no 11B, p 7223.

186 Fletcher, K. and Tripp, C. (1994) *Focus on communication*, Denver: Denver Public Schools Co.

187 Fox, R.W. (1983) 'The effects of a residential basic counseling skills training program', *Dissertation Abstracts International*, vol 43, no 7A, p 2236.

188 Frazier, M.E. (1986) 'Teaching relationship enhancement skills to hospice professionals', *Dissertation Abstracts International*, vol 46, no 9A, p 2593.

189 Gallagher, C.A. (1993) 'Empathy and assertiveness training in a nursing home environment', *Dissertation Abstracts International*, vol 54, no 4B, p 2239.

190 Gerrard, B.A. (1983) 'The outcomes of a comprehensive interpersonal skills programme for health professionals', *Dissertation Abstracts International*, vol 44, no 2B, p 607.

191 Gibbs, P.A. (1982) 'A descriptive study on the use of educational drama techniques to develop empathy in social work students', *Dissertation Abstracts International*, vol 43, no 3A, p 647.

192 Gillotti, C., Thompson, T. and McNeilis, K. (2002) 'Communicative competence in the delivery of bad news', *Social Science & Medicine*, vol 54, no 7, pp 1011-24.

193 Goldberg, S., Cullen, J. and Austin, M.J. (2001) 'Developing a public information and community relations strategy in a county social service agency', *Administration in Social Work*, vol 25, no 2, pp 61-79.

194 Hall, D., James, P. and Roberts, S. (1997) 'Evaluation of training in behaviour change counselling skills: the application of clinical–audit methodology', *Health Education Journal*, vol 56, no 4, pp 393-403.

195 Hanlon, J.M. (1996) 'Teaching effective communication skills', *Nursing Management*, vol 27, no 4, pp 48B, 48D.

196 Harris, H. (1986) 'Hospice training teaches communication', *Texas Hospitals*, vol 41, no 9, pp 20-1.

197 Hirsch, G. and Altman, K. (1986) 'Training graduate students in parent conference skills', *Applied Research in Mental Retardation*, vol 7, no 3, pp 371-85.

198 Huddleston, D. and Alexander, R. (1999) 'Communicating in end–of–life care', *Caring*, vol 18, no 2, pp 16-17.

199 Hunsdon, S. (1984) 'The impact of illness on patients and families: social workers teach medical students', *Social Work in Health Care*, vol 10, no 2, pp 41-52.

200 Itzhaky, H. (1987) 'Social work supervision as a basis for communication and innovation', *Journal of Social Work and Policy in Israel*, vol 1, pp 65-77.

201 Jacobs, J.J. (1982) 'The development of communication skills in social work by means of laboratory work', *Dissertation Abstracts International*, vol 42, no 9A, p 4152.

202 Kelley, P. (1995) 'Integrating narrative approaches into clinical curricula: addressing diversity through understanding', *Journal of Social Work Education*, vol 31, no 3, pp 347-57.

203 Kinseth, L.M. (1989) 'Nonverbal training for psychotherapy: overcoming barriers to clinical work with client nonverbal behavior', *The Clinical Supervisor*, vol 7, no 1, pp 5-25.

204 Kramer, J.R. and Reitz, M. (1980) 'Using video playback to train family therapists', *Family Process*, vol 19, no 2, pp 145-50.

205 Lewis, L.F., Garcia, J.E. and Hallock, A.L. (2002) 'Applying group support systems in social work education and practice', *Journal of Technology in Human Services*, vol 20, no 1/2, pp 201-25.

206 Lindsey, E.W., Kropf, N.P. and Carse, M.S. (1995) 'Training public assistance workers in policy and interpersonal helping skills', *Research on Social Work Practice*, vol 5, no 1, pp 20-35.

207 McArdle, G.K. and McDermott, M.R. (1994) 'From directive expert to non-directive partner: a study of facilitating change in the occupational self-perceptions of health visitors and schools nurses', *British Journal of Guidance and Counselling*, vol 22, no 1, pp 107-17.

208 McCallion, P., Toseland, R.W., Lacey, D. and Banks, S. (1999) 'Educating nursing assistants to communicate more effectively with nursing home residents with dementia', *Gerontologist*, vol 39, no 5, pp 546-58.

209 McGrath, P., Yates, P., Clinton, M. and Hart, G. (1999) '"What should I say?": qualitative findings on dilemmas in palliative care nursing', *Hospice Journal*, vol 14, no 2, pp 17-33.

210 Main, F.O., Boughner, S.R., Mims, G.A. and Schieffer, J.L. (2001) 'Rolling the dice: an experiential exercise for enhancing interventive counseling skill', *Family Journal Counseling and Therapy for Couples and Families*, vol 9, no 4, pp 450-4.

211 Malikiosi, L.M., Mehnert, W.O., Work, G.G. and Gold, J. (1981) 'Differential supervision and cognitive structure effects on empathy and counseling effectiveness', *International Journal for the Advancement of Counselling*, vol 4, no 2, pp 119-29.

212 Malon, D.W. and Spencer, D.M. (1985) 'Continuity and discontinuity in family therapy training', *Journal of Social Work Education*, vol 21, no 1, pp 66-73.

213 Martin, M.E., Pine, B.A. and Healy, L.M. (1999) 'Mining our strengths: curriculum approaches in social work management', *Journal of Teaching in Social Work*, vol 18, no 1/2, pp 73-97.

214 Mason, L. (1998) 'Fieldwork education: collaborative group learning in community settings', *Australian Occupational Therapy Journal*, vol 45, no 4, pp 124-30.

215 Miller, M.W. (1982) 'Professional/client interaction: implications for education and management', *Dissertation Abstracts International*, vol 42, no 12B, Pt 1, p 4746.

216 Myer, D.F. (1983) *Interpersonal communication: Techniques and style. An instructor resource guide. Appendix to a Final Report on the Paraprofessional Rurally Oriented Family Home Health Training Program*, Charleston: Baptist College.

217 Nemeth, E. and Kolozsi, B. (1999) 'Communication and social skills training for peer helpers: an East European program', *Administration & Policy in Mental Health*, vol 26, no 5, pp 373-5.

218 Norris, J.F. (1985) 'Lecture and role play instruction for communication skills: an analysis of the influence of student attributes and teaching strategy on learning outcomes', *Dissertation Abstracts International*, vol 45, no 12A, p 3535.

219 Orr, D.P. and Vickery, M.L. (1983) 'A values clarification workshop experience for residents', *Journal of Adolescent Health Care*, vol 3, no 4, pp 256-63.

220 Peloquin, S.M. (1995) 'Communication skills: why not turn to a skills training model?', *American Journal of Occupational Therapy*, vol 49, no 7, pp 721-3.

221 Pilkington, W.J. (1993) *Effects of a communication program on nursing home staff's attitudes and communication skills and residents' levels of life satisfaction*, New York, NY: St John's University, p 111.

222 Pillemer, K., Hegeman, C.R., Albright, B. and Henderson, C. (1998) 'Building bridges between families and nursing home staff: the Partners in Caregiving program', *Gerontologist*, vol 38, no 4, pp 499-503.

223 Prescott, P., Opheim, A. and Bortveit, T. (2002) 'Effekten av kurs og opperlaering i radgivningsferdigheter/The effect of workshops and training on counseling skills', *Tidsskrift for Norsk Psykologforening*, vol 39, no 5, pp 426-31.

224 Ramsay, J.A. (1984) 'A brief note on unobtrusive observation of an encounter group', *Small Group Behavior*, vol 15, no 3, pp 414-16.

225 Rodway, M. and Wright, M. (1988) 'Sociopsychological aspects of sexually transmitted diseases', *Journal of Social Work and Human Sexuality*, vol 6, no 2, whole issue.

[226] Rose, S.D. (1988) 'Practice experiments for doctoral dissertations: research training and knowledge building', *Journal of Social Work Education*, vol 24, pp 115-22.

[227] Rushton, A. and Nathan, J. (1996) 'The supervision of child protection work', *British Journal of Social Work*, vol 26, no 3, pp 357-74.

[228] Russell-Chapin, L.A. and Sherman, N.E. (2000) 'The counselling interview rating form: a teaching and evaluation tool for counsellor education', *British Journal of Guidance and Counselling*, vol 28, no 1, pp 115-24.

[229] Rustomfram, N. (1991) 'Training for communication skills – implications for community education', *Source Indian Journal of Social Work*, vol 52, pp 303-12.

[230] Scharlach, A.E. (1985) 'Social group work with institutionalized elders: a task-centered approach', *Social Work with Groups*, vol 8, no 3, pp 33-47.

[231] Seabury, B. (1994) 'Interactive video disc programs in social work education: "crisis counseling" and "organizational assessment"', *Computers in Human Services*, vol 11, no 3-4, pp 299-316.

[232] Seabury, B.A. (2002) 'COW: conferencing on the web', *Journal of Technology in Human Services*, vol 20, no 3/4, pp 231-44.

[233] Seabury, B.-A. and Maple, Jr, F.-F. (1993) 'Using computers to teach practice skills', *Social-Work*, vol 38, no 4, pp 430-9.

[234] Shaw, D. and May, H. (2001) 'Sharing knowledge with nursing home staff: an objective investigation', *International Journal of Language and Communication Disorders*, vol 36, Supplement, pp 200-5.

[235] Slayer, D. and Courtney, J. (1996) 'Communication skills in interpersonal relations', National Educational Video, Inc, Naples (www.nevcoeducation.com).

[236] Smettem, S. (1999) 'Welcome/Assalaam-u-alaikaam: improving communications with ethnic minority families', *Paediatric Nursing*, vol 11, no 2, pp 33-5.

[237] Spielberg, G. (1980) 'Graduate training in helping relationships: helpful or harmful?', *Journal of Humanistic Psychology*, vol 20, no 3, pp 57-70.

[238] Stanley, N. and Manthorpe, J. (2001) 'Reading mental health inquiries: messages for social work full text delivery', *Journal of social work*, vol 1, no 1, pp 77-100.

[239] Texas Consortium of Geriatric Education Centers (1993) *Educational resource manual for Baccalaureate social work field instruction in gerontology*, Houston, Texas Consortium of Geriatric Education Centers.

[240] Vocational Education Services (1985) *Nursing assistants for long-term care. Performance-based instructional materials*, Bloomington:Vocational Education Services, Indiana University.

[241] Wodarski, J.S., Pippin, J.A. and Daniels, M. (1988) 'The effects of graduate social work education on personality, values and interpersonal skills', *Journal of Social Work Education*, vol 24, no 3, pp 266-77.

[242] Wortman, J. (1990) 'Empathy and social work: the capacity of students for cognitive and emotional empathy as it relates to field instruction evaluations', *Dissertation Abstracts International A*, vol 51, no 4, pp 1392-3.

[243] Jessup, H. and Rogerson, S. (1999) op cit, p 161.

[244] Marsh, P. and Treseliotis, J. (1996) op cit, p 203.

[245] Marsh, P. and Treseliotis, J. (1996) op cit, p 220.

[246] Kadushin, A. and Kadushin, G. (1997) op cit, p 27.

[247] Randall, R. and Parker, J. (2000) 'Communication theory', in M. Davies, *Blackwell encyclopaedia of social work*, Oxford: Oxford University Press, p 69.

[248] GSCC (General Social Care Council) (2002) *Assuring quality for the diploma in social work - 1. Rules and requirements for the DipSW*, London: GSCC, p 15.

[249] NAW (2003) op cit, p 6.

[250] QAA (2000) op cit, p 12.

[251] Trevithick, P. (2003) 'Social work skills, abilities and skill transferability: the importance of the relationship between theory and practice', unpublished paper, University of Bristol.

[252] Lishman, J. (1994) op cit, p 53.

[253] Shulman, L. (1999) *The skills of helping. Individuals, groups and communities*, Illinois: Peacock, p 156.

[254] Croft, S. and Beresford, P. (2000) 'Empowerment', in M. Davies, *Blackwell encyclopaedia of social work*, Oxford: Oxford University Press, p 116.

[255] Barker, R.L. (1999) *The social work dictionary*, Maryland: NASW Press, p 153.

[256] McIvor, G. (2000) 'The evaluation of effectiveness', in M. Davies, *Blackwell encyclopaedia of social work*, Oxford: Oxford University Press, p 121.

[257] Macdonald, G. (2000) 'Evidence-based practice', in M. Davies, *Blackwell encyclopaedia of social work*, Oxford: Oxford University Press, p 123.

[258] Barker, R.L. (1999) op cit, p 190.

[259] Barker, R.L. (1999) op cit, p 192.

[260] Parsloe, P. (2000) 'Generic and specialist practice', in M. Davies, *Blackwell encyclopaedia of social work*, Oxford: Oxford University Press, p 145.

[261]   Gambrill, E. (1997) *Social work practice: A critical thinker's guide*, Oxford: Oxford University Press, p 309.

[262]   Kennard, D., Roberts, J. and Winter, D.A. (1993) *A workbook of group-analytic interventions*, London: Routledge, p 3.

[263]   Barker, R.L. (1999) op cit, p 252.

[264]   Kadushin, A. and Kadushin, G. (1997) op cit, p 14.

[265]   Kadushin, A. and Kadushin, G. (1997) op cit, p 3.

[266]   O'Hagan, K. (1996) op cit, p 8.

[267]   Clark, C. (2000) 'The use of language', in M. Davies, *Blackwell encyclopaedia of social work*, Oxford: Oxford University Press, p 181.

[268]   Montgomery, M. (1995) *An introduction to language and society*, London: Routledge, cited in N. Thompson (2003, p 36)[105].

[269]   QAA (2000) op cit, p 17.

[270]   Kolb, D.A. (1984) op cit, p 38.

[271]   Kolb, D.A. (1984) op cit, p 41.

[272]   Egan, G. (1990) op cit, p 108.

[273]   Kadushin, A. and Kadushin, G. (1997) op cit, p 50.

[274]   Egan, G. (1990) op cit, p 111.

[275]   Barker, R.L. (1999) op cit, p 285.

[276]   Barker, R.L. (1999) op cit, p 302.

[277]   Lishman, J. (1994) op cit, p 20.

[278]   Kadushin, A. and Kadushin, G. (1997) op cit, pp 289-308.

[279]   Kadushin, A. and Kadushin, G. (1997) op cit, p 315.

[280]   Gambrill, E. (1997) op cit, p 375.

[281]   QAA (2000) op cit, p 14-15.

[282]   Gambrill, E. (1997) op cit, p 101.

[283]   Cournoyer, B. (2000) op cit, p 5.

[284]   Barker, R.L. (1999) op cit, p 130.

[285]   Sheldon, B. (2000) 'Cognitive behavioural methods in social care: a look at the evidence', in P. Stepney and D. Ford, *Social work models, methods and theories*, Lyme Regis: Russell House Publishers, pp 74-6.

[286]   QAA (2000) op cit, p 13-14.

[287]   Barker, R.L. (1999) p 485.

[288]   Trevithick, P. (2000) op cit, p 13.

[289]   Parsloe, P. (1988) 'Developing interviewing skills', *Social Work Education*, vol 8, no 1, pp 3-9 [p 8].

[290]   Gambrill, E. (1997) op cit, p 173.

Search strategy

The search strategy was written up by Wendy Hardyman (SCIE) in collaboration with the authors of this review and CRD.

Sources

The literature was identified for the research review from a number of sources:

- electronic databases
- handsearching
- personal libraries of the Working Group.

The focus of the review was on learning and teaching of communication skills in social work education. It was, however, acknowledged that literature from professions outside of social work/social care may also be of relevance, such as nursing or medicine/allied professions.

Some preliminary searching was conducted by a research analyst at SCIE, prior to the CRD work commencing, in order both to identify key literature and to explore the utility of various search terms. This was using the search terms below.

(communication skills train* or communication skill* or communication)

AND

(teach* or learn* or assess* or eval*)

AND

(social work education or social work or social care or health or nurs*)

Combinations including the term 'communication' only led to very large numbers of records being identified, particularly in the healthcare literature. Details of these searches and examples of relevant records identified from preliminary searching were made available to CRD, to assist in finalising the search criteria and to help identify which electronic databases should be searched.

Electronic database search

The main literature search for the research review was conducted by CRD. Bibliographic databases covering social work, social sciences and health literature were searched in order to assess the size of the literature for this scoping review. The strategy was developed using Sociological Abstracts and MEDLINE databases. No language limits were applied, but because of changes in social work education over the years literature published before 1982 was excluded as it was agreed that it was unlikely to be currently relevant. It was anticipated that there would be little literature specifically related to social work; it was therefore decided to widen the search to include health professionals.

A series of preliminary strategies were carried out on both Sociological Abstracts and MEDLINE, and a sample number of references retrieved were assessed by the Working Group. Although the main focus of interest was on education, the Working Group decided that papers relating to communication and interpersonal skills with particular client groups provided a framework for understanding, and approaches to training and might therefore be useful. This resulted in a broader approach being adopted for the search strategy, which retrieved a high number of records particularly on the medical databases.

In order to keep the number of records to a manageable level the strategy was adapted for the medical databases. This entailed (a) removing some of the subject headings, which were increasing the number of irrelevant references, (b) linking the concepts of teaching or learning with the communication skills terms, and (c) using word adjacency within the teaching/learning facet with the concepts of evaluation or competencies in order to improve the specificity of the search. For the non-medical databases, a broader strategy was adopted by combining communication terms with teaching/learning terms and social work or allied health groups.

The results from each search were entered into an electronic reference library (Endnote) and duplicate records removed.

The following databases were searched between 12/03/03 and 03/04/03.

Table 1: Databases searched

Social Work Abstracts 1982-2002/12	CINAHL 1982-2003
ASSIA 1987-2003/03	Cochrane Library Issue 1 2003
SIGLE 1980-2002/12	Sociological Abstracts 1982-2002/12
Wilson Social Science Abstracts 1982-2003	ERIC 1982-2003/3
Social SciSearch 1982-2003/03	MEDLINE 1982-2003/3
IBSS 1982-2003/03	[a]CareData 1982-2003
British Education Index 1982-2002/11	Dissertation Abstracts 1982-2003
PsycINFO 1982-2003/3	HMIC 1982-2003
British Nursing Index 1994-2003	

Note: [a] CareData was searched using the SCIE in-house interface in order to permit more complex searching than otherwise available via Internet access.

Hand searching

CRD provided a frequency distribution of the journals in which records identified as relevant were published. A decision was made to search electronically available online contents (abstracts/papers) for the period January 2002 to the present day for the 10 most frequently sourced journals.

The top 10 journals and the issues that were searched are outlined below. Please note that hard copies of journals were not searched; it was only electronic versions that were accessed. All online searches were conducted on Tuesday 10 June 2003.

Table 2: Hand searched electronic journals

Journal title	Volume, issue, year searched online
Journal of Education for Social Work/ Journal of Social Work Education[a]	vol 38, 1-3, 2002
Journal of Teaching in Social Work	vol 22, 1-4, 2002
Journal of Technology in Human Services	vol 21, 3, 2002
	vol 20, 1-4, 2002
	vol 19, 1-3, 2002
British Journal of Social Work	vol 33, 1-3, 2003
	vol 32, 1-8, 2002
Computers in Human Services	DISCONTINUED
Journal of Continuing Social Work Education	NO ONLINE VERSION AVAILABLE
Canadian Social Work Review	vol 19, 1, 2002
International Journal of Language and Communication Disorders	vol 38, 1-2, 2003
	vol 37, 1-4, 2002
International Social Work	vol 46, 1, 2003
	vol 45, 1-4, 2002

Note: [a] These are the same journal now.

Authors' personal libraries

In addition to the records identified from the electronic search, texts and journal papers were also identified from the authors' personal libraries. The number of additional papers and texts retrieved through this method is reported in the section below.

Preliminary coding and inclusion criteria

Records to be deemed as relevant for the search were those that were about improving the communication skills of social care professionals and learning/teaching. In order to identify these records, a coding strategy was developed (see Figure 1 for details). This enabled the literature to be mapped. The preliminary phase of the coding was to ascertain whether records were about (a) learning and teaching of communication skills and improving the skill of professionals, (b) learning and teaching of communication skills and improving the skills of service users or (c) general papers on communication. For those papers that were classified as being about learning and teaching of communication skills and improving the skills of professionals, a further level of coding was applied, in order to identify professional grouping, that is, (i) social work/social care, (ii) allied professions, for example, counselling and (iii) nursing/ medicine. It was acknowledged that some papers may be multi-disciplinary in nature and apply to more than one grouping.

The majority of coding was undertaken by CRD, who coded all records identified from the electronic database search. Where there was uncertainty about coding, a cautious approach was adopted. This led to a higher number of papers being identified as relevant at this preliminary phase of coding than was otherwise found to be the case once abstracts were reviewed by the Working Group. Details are reported in the section below.

A further category of papers was also identified, this being those papers that were about improving the communication skills of professionals which, although they did not report directly on the learning and teaching of communication skills, had possible implications for practice.

The purpose of the detailed coding is to enable further work to be undertaken at a later date on those records deemed as of secondary but important relevance, for example, the literature exploring learning and teaching of communication skills in related fields, that is, allied professions and nursing/medicine, and the literature pertaining to the improvement of communication skills in service users.

Data recording and quality appraisal

Information and quality appraisal on the studies/papers included was recorded using form 1 and 2 (see end of this Appendix).

Quality appraisal was undertaken by considering the following aspects of each study:

• aim of study;
• research, type, sample, methods;
• student and/or service user participation;

- key messages/findings;
- relevance of research to learning and teaching of qualifying social work programmes;
- application/do-ability;
- overall strengths and weaknesses/appropriateness of methods employed.

Two members of the Working Group took responsibility for reviewing abstracts identified from the electronic database search. Each reviewed 50% of abstracts; where abstracts were excluded these were read and discussed by both reviewers. References identified from other sources, such as hand searching, were read by one member of the Working Group.

Results

The results of the various search strategies are also charted in Figure 2.

It was originally anticipated that this review would draw on the literature in fields other than social work/social care, hence the search strategy being designed to capture literature in nursing/medicine and allied professions to social work/social care. However, given the vast the number of records retrieved (as detailed below), only the literature concerning learning and teaching of communication skills in social work/ social care will be considered in this review. Examination of development in other fields are seen as separate and additional pieces of work.

Preliminary scoping

This led to the retrieval of 16 potentially relevant papers, of which 11 were also identified and coded as relevant in the York CRD search and full papers sent to members of the Working Group. Four of the papers not coded as of direct relevance were also identified in the preliminary scoping, but were coded by the reviewers at York as either (a) not of relevance ($n=2$) or (b) of possible relevance ($n=2$), as although they discussed improving communication skills of professionals, they did not directly focus on learning and teaching. These four papers were not included in the review. One of the two papers identified from scoping but not present in the York search was included in the review[103].

Electronic databases

A total of **8,023** records were retrieved from the search conducted by CRD. These were coded according to the strategy outlined above. This led to the following breakdown (see Table 3).

Table 3: Search results from electronic databases

Database	Total citations	Duplicates	Total unique citations
Social Work Abstracts	482	8	474
ASSIA	492	47	445
SIGLE	22	2	20
Wilson Social Science Abstracts	2	2	1
Social SciSearch	22	12	10
IBSS	72	12	60
British Education Index	32	13	19
PsychINFO	1,777	143	1,634
HMIC	413	104	309
BNI	67	23	44
CINAHL	1,078	162	916
Cochrane Library	199	112	87
Sociological Abstracts	439	439	392
ERIC	1,340	116	1,224
MEDLINE	3,004	869	2,135
CareData	305	56	249
Dissertation Abstracts	4	0	4
Total	**9,751**	**1,728**	**8,023**

Note references were deduplicated manually and also using EndNote. However, many more were identified manually. From the deduplication it was noted that that there was a lot of duplicates between Social Work Abstracts and Sociological Abstracts, between PsycINFO and ERIC, and between CINAHL, MEDLINE and the Cochrane Controlled Trials Register (CCTR) on Cochrane Library.

A total of 149 out of the 8,023 records (excluding duplicates) were preliminarily coded as of primary relevance. Preliminary reading of abstracts from the electronic database search led to 68 relevant records being identified, which was increased to 79 when reviewers discussed excluded abstracts. Of these 79, 6 were theses, 14 texts and 57 papers. An additional journal article was also included from the York database search, which had originally not been coded as relevant due to lack of information in the abstract. The rationale for including this extra reference was that it was a publication arising from one of the 6 theses that were deemed as relevant. The total number of records therefore deemed as relevant from the electronic database search was 80 (6 theses, 14 texts and 60 papers) out of a possible 150.

A decision was made **not** to include the 6 theses in the research review, mainly due to difficulties obtaining these and the time the theses were undertaken. Three records were also excluded as the papers did not arrive in time for the write-up of the review[180, 200, 209], leaving 73 records. A further 12 records were excluded on retrieval/reading of the full papers as they were not deemed relevant. Following a two-stage process for assessing the relevance of these records, the total number included in the review from the electronic search totalled 59 (45 papers and 14 texts). A further 4 papers were identified through hand searching, of which 2 were included in the review process and an additional 20 texts, 1 report text, 3 journal papers (1 of these from the preliminary scoping exercise[78]) and 1 e-learning package from authors' personal libraries. (See 'Results' and Figure 2, for a detailed write-up of results.) The total number of records included in this review from the various search strategies was 86 records – 50 papers, 34 texts, 1 report and 1 e-learning package.

Three of the texts included in the review had later editions published than the search identified[28,37,51]. It was agreed that these later texts should be used in the review and counted as part of the York database search. In relation to Egan, the York database search only identified one text – the 1985 edition of the training manual for Egan's text, *The skilled helper*. For consistency, the latest edition of the training manual is counted as part of the York search[38]. The latest edition of *The skilled helper*[37] is also cited in as an included text. An exception to this is in Appendix C, where specific quotes from an earlier edition of *The skilled helper*[149] have been cited.

Excluded records

The papers excluded at the initial reading of abstract stage, and the subsequent full reading stage, fell into two broad categories: either they did not directly relate to the social work profession and/or they were not specifically about the learning and teaching of communication skills in social work education. A full list of all the excluded records can be found in the reference section[150-242].

Table 4 below details number of relevant records identified per database.

Table 4: Relevant records per database

Social Work Abstracts – 15 records	CINAHL – 1 record
PsycINFO – 11 records	IBSS – 1 record
ASSIA – 8 records	MEDLINE – 1 record
CareData – 8 records	Wilson Social Science Abstracts – 0 records
Sociological Abstracts – 6 records	Cochrane Library – 0 records
ERIC – 3 records	Dissertation Abstracts – 0 records
Social SciSearch – 2 records	British Education Index – 0 records
HMIC – 2 records	SIGLE – 0 records
British Nursing Index – 1 record	

Authors' personal libraries

An additional 20 texts[37,42-5,54-6,58,62,66,81,83,84,86,87,92,94,123,133] and 1 report were identified as of relevance to the review from authors' personal libraries. While some of these texts were published outside of the timeframe used for the purposes of this review, they were considered to be important texts which needed to be referred to in order to contextualise the reviewed literature. (The report cited is as yet an unpublished report[33].)

Two additional papers were included from authors' personal libraries[71,77] and 1 e-learning package, Procare[52].

Hand searching

This strategy led to the retrieval of 4 further relevant papers[60,64,205,232], of which 2[60,64] were included in the literature search once full papers were read and appraised.

Results of all searches

Results of all searches identified a total of 86 records[5,12,15-98] – 50 papers, 34 texts, 1 report and 1 e-learning package – as of relevance to the review.

Further coding

Six members of the communications Working Group took responsibility for reading and analysis of papers/texts and so on, with two members working on theoretical literature, two on narrative and evaluative literature and two on specialised literature:

- *theoretical:* papers/texts addressing theoretical frameworks informing learning and teaching communication skills;
- *narrative:* papers providing detailed descriptions of design and content of skills training programmes, no systematic evaluation;
- *evaluative:* papers with limited description of programme content and rationale, focus on measurement of outcomes;
- *specialised:* papers addressing learning and teaching of specialised communication skills;
- *combined:* papers covering more than one of the above definitional categories.

The breakdown of coding of these **86** total records was as follows:

59 records from electronic database search:

- 17 theoretical
- 18 evaluative/narrative
- 11 specialised

- 11 combined theoretical/evaluative/narrative
- 2 evaluative/narrative/specialised.

2 records from hand searching:

- 1 theoretical/narrative
- 1 evaluative.

25 records – authors' personal libraries/preliminary scoping.

The coding of these records was more complex, with 20 texts and 1 report covering some elements of all aspects of the coding classification:

- 21 combined theoretical/narrative/specialised/evaluative
- 1 evaluative/narrative
- 2 narrative
- 1 specialised.

Figure 1:Coding strategy

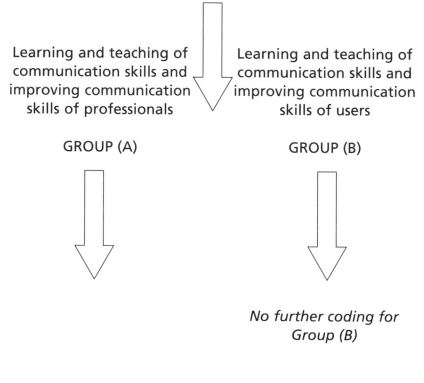

PRIMARY FILTER/CODING

Learning and teaching of communication skills and improving communication skills of professionals

Learning and teaching of communication skills and improving communication skills of users

GROUP (A)

GROUP (B)

No further coding for Group (B)

SECONDARY FILTER/CODING FOR GROUP (A)

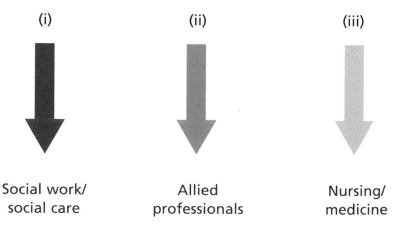

(i)

(ii)

(iii)

Social work/ social care

Allied professionals

Nursing/ medicine

Figure 2: Breakdown of records identified from search strategy

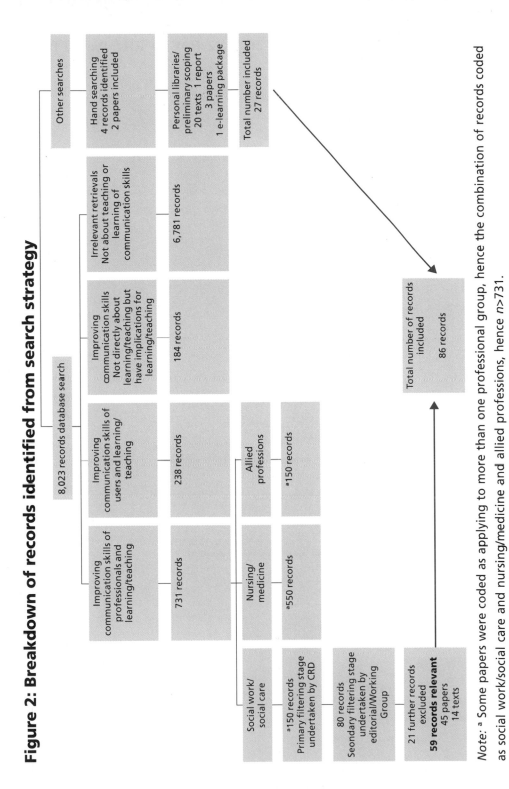

Note: [a] Some papers were coded as applying to more than one professional group, hence the combination of records coded as social work/social care and nursing/medicine and allied professions, hence *n>731*.

Social Work Abstracts 1982-2002/12 (OVID ERL WebSPIRS)
Searched 12.3.03

#1   nonverbal-communication in DE

#2   (interpersonal-communication in DE) or (interpersonal-communication-training in DE)

#3   (interpersonal-skill-training in DE) or (interpersonal-skills-training in DE)

#4   empathy in DE

#5   (counseling) or (counselling in DE)

#6   communication in DE

#7   (communicat* near3 skill*) in ti,ab

#8   (communicat* near3 competen*) in ti,ab

#9   (communicat* near3 improve*) in ti,ab

#10 (communicat* near3 improving) in ti,ab

#11 (communicat* near3 enhanc*) in ti,ab

#12 (communicat* near3 develop*) in ti,ab

#13 (effective* near3 communicat*) in ti,ab

#14 cst in ti,ab

#15 (interpersonal near3 skill*) in ti,ab

#16 (interpersonal near3 communicat*) in ti,ab

#17 (consultation* near3 skill*) in ti,ab

#18 (consulting near3 skill*) in ti,ab

#19 ((counseling or counselling) near3 skill*) in ti,ab

#20 (listen* near3 skill*) in ti,ab

#21 (listen* near3 develop*) in ti,ab

#22 (empath* near3 communicat*) in ti,ab

#23 (empath* near3 skill*) in ti,ab

#24 (interprofession* near3 communicat*) in ti,ab

#25 #1 or #2 or #3 or #4 or #5 or #6 or #7 or #8 or #9 or #10 or #11 or #12 or #13 or #14 or #15 or #16 or #17 or #18 or #19 or #20 or #21 or #22 or #23 or #24

#26 educational-programs in DE

#27 courses in DE

#28 seminars- in DE

#29 vocational-education in DE

#30 job-training in DE

#31 professional-education in DE

#32 program-evaluation in DE

#33 undergraduate-education in DE

#34 higher-education in DE

#35 adult-education in DE

#36 learning in DE

#37 curriculum in DE

#38 social-work-education in DE

#39 social-work-students in DE

#40 professional-education in DE

#41 (training or trained or trainer* or train) in ti,ab

#42 (course* or workshop* or work-shop* or program or programs or programme*) in ti,ab

#43 (educat* or pedagog*)in ti,ab

#44 (teach* or taught or instruction* or tuition* or supervis*) in ti,ab

#45 (tutor* or facilitat*) in ti,ab

#46 (learn* or curriculum or curricula*) in ti,ab

#47 (classes or lecture* or seminar*) in ti,ab

#48 #26 or #27 or #28 or #29 or #30 or #31 or #32 or #33 or #34 or #35 or #36 or #37 or #38 or #39 or #40 or #41 or #42 or #43 or #44 or #45 or #46 or #47

#49 #25 and #48

****

Sociological Abstracts 1986–2002/12 (ARC Silverplatter) Searched 12.3.03

#1   "Verbal-Communication" in DE

#2   "Nonverbal-Communication" in DE

#3   «Interpersonal-Communication» in DE

#4   "Empathy-" in DE

#5   "Counseling-" in DE

#6   (communicat* near3 skill*) in ti,ab

#7   (communicat* near3 competen*) in ti,ab

#8   (communicat* near3 improve*) in ti,ab

#9   (communicat* near3 improving) in ti,ab

#10 (communicat* near3 enhanc*) in ti,ab

#11 (communicat* near3 develop*) in ti,ab

#12 (effective* near3 communicat*) in ti,ab

#13 cst in ti,ab

#14 (interpersonal near3 skill*) in ti,ab

#15 (interpersonal near3 communicat*) in ti,ab
#16 (consultation* near3 skill*) in ti,ab
#17 (consulting near3 skill*) in ti,ab
#18 ((counseling or counselling) near3 skill*) in ti,ab
#19 (listen* near3 skill*) in ti,ab
#20 (listen* near3 develop*) in ti,ab
#21 (empath* near3 communicat*) in ti,ab
#22 (empath* near3 skill*) in ti,ab
#23 (interprofession* near3 communicat*) in ti,ab
#24 #1 or #2 or #3 or #4 or #5 or #6 or #7 or #8 or #9 or #10 or #11 or #12 or #13 or #14 or #15 or #16 or #17 or #18 or #19 or #20 or #21 or #22 or #23
#25 "Educational-Programs" in DE
#26 "Courses-" in DE
#27 "seminars" in DE
#28 "Vocational-Education" in DE
#29 "Job-Training" in DE
#30 "Professional-Training" in DE
#31 "Occupational-Qualifications" in DE
#32 «Program-Evaluation» in DE
#33 "Teacher-Evaluation" in DE
#34 "Student-Evaluation" in DE
#35 explode "Academic-Degrees"
#36 "Undergraduate-Programs" in DE
#37 "Higher-Education" in DE
#38 "Adult-Education" in DE
#39 "Learning-" in DE
#40 "Curriculum-" in DE
#41 (training or trained or trainer* or train) in ti,ab
#42 (course* or workshop* or work-shop* or program or programs or programme*) in ti,ab
#43 (educat* or pedagog*) in ti,ab
#44 (teach* or taught or instruction* or tuition* or supervis*) in ti,ab
#45 (tutor* or facilitat*) in ti,ab
#46 (learn* or curriculum or curricula*) in ti,ab
#47 (classes or lecture* or seminar*) in ti,ab
#48 #25 or #26 or #27 or #28 or #29 or #30 or #31 or #32 or #33 or #34 or #35 or #36 or #37 or #38 or #39 or #40 or #41 or #42 or #43 or #44 or #45 or #46 or #47

#49 "Social-Work" in DE

#50 "Social-Work-Education" in DE

#51 "Midwifery-" in DE

#52 "Pharmacy-" in DE

#53 "Physicians-" in DE

#54 "Paramedical-Personnel" in DE

#55 "Health-Professions" in DE

#56 "Medical-Schools" in DE

#57 "Medical-Students" in DE

#58 explode "Medicine"

#59 (social work*) in ti,ab

#60 (nurse or nurses or nursing) in ti,ab

#61 (health visitor*) in ti,ab

#62 (midwif* or midwive*) in ti,ab

#63 (pharmacy or pharmacist*) in ti,ab

#64 (health professional* or health practitioner*) in ti,ab

#65 (medical or medic or medics or clinical) in ti,ab

#66 (doctor* or gp or gps or general practitioner* or family practitioner* or primary care practitioner* or physician*) in ti,ab

#67 #49 or #50 or #51 or #52 or #53 or #54 or #55 or #56 or #57 or #58 or #59 or #60 or #61 or #62 or #63 or #64 or #65 or #66

#68 #24 and #48

#69 #68 and #67

****

ASSIA (Applied Social Science Index & Abstracts) 1987–2003 (Cambridge Scientific Abstracts) Searched 12.3.03

OR   (de=((facilitated communication)))

OR   Explode ((de=((nonverbal communication))))

OR   Explode ((de=((communication skills)))

OR   (de=((communication skills training)))

OR   (de=((empathy)))

OR   (de=((counselling)))

OR   (ab=(communicat* within 3 skill*))

OR   (ti=(communicat* within 3 skill*))

OR   (ab=(communicat* within 3 competen*))

OR (ti=(communicat* within 3 competen*))
OR (ab=(communicat* within 3 improve*))
OR (ti=(communicat* within 3 improve*))
OR (ab=(communicat* within 3 improving))
OR (ti=(communicat* within 3 improving))
OR (ab=(communicat* within 3 enhanc*))
OR (ti=(communicat* within 3 enhanc*))
OR (ab=(communicat* within 3 develop*))
OR (ti=(communicat* within 3 develop*))
OR (ab=(effective* within 3 communicat*))
OR (ti=(effective* within 3 communicat*))
OR (ti=cst)
OR (ab=(interpersonal within 3 skill*))
OR (ti=(interpersonal within 3 skill*))
OR (ti=(interpersonal within 3 communicat*))
OR (ab=(interpersonal within 3 communicat*))
OR (ab=(consultation* within 3 skill*))
OR (ti=(consultation* within 3 skill*))
OR (ab=(consulting within 3 skill*))
OR (ti=(consulting within 3 skill*))
OR (ab=(counsel*ing within 3 skill*))
OR (ti=(counsel*ing within 3 skill*))
OR (ab=(listen* within 3 skill*))
OR (ti=(listen* within 3 skill*))
OR (ab=(listen* within 3 develop*))
OR (ti=(listen* within 3 develop*))
OR (ab=(empath* within 3 communicat*))
OR (ti=(empath* within 3 communicat*))
OR (ab=(empath* within 3 skill*))
OR (ti=(empath* within 3 skill*))
OR ((ab=(interprofession* within 3 communicat*))
OR (ti=(interprofession* within 3 communicat*))

AND

OR (de=((teacher-student interactions)))
OR (de=((trainer-trainee interactions)))
OR (de=((professional training)))
OR (de=((vocational education)))

OR (de=((seminars)))
OR ((de=((courses) or (modular courses) or (short courses))))
OR (de=((educational programmes))))
OR (de=((adult education)))
OR (de=((higher education)))
OR Explode ((de=((learning)
OR (de=((degrees)))
OR (de=((curriculum)))
OR (ab=(training or trained or trainer* or train))
OR (ti=(training or trained or trainer* or train))
OR (ab=(educat* or pedagog*))
OR (ti=(educat* or pedagog*))
OR (ab=(course* or workshop* or program or programs or programme*))
OR (ti=(course* or workshop* or program or programs or programme*))
OR (ab=(teach* or taught or instruction* or tuition* or supervis*))
OR (ti=(teach* or taught or instruction* or tuition* or supervis*))
OR (ab=(tutor* or facilitat*))
OR (ti=(tutor* or facilitat*))
OR (ab=(learn* or curriculum or curricula*))
OR   (ti=(learn* or curriculum or curricula*))
OR (((ab=(classes or lecture* or seminar*))
OR (ti=(classes or lecture* or seminar*))

AND

OR Explode ((de=((social work)
OR (de=((medical schools)))
OR (de=((midwifery)))
OR Explode ((de=((midwives))
OR Explode ((de=((nursing))
OR Explode((de=((nurses)
OR Explode ((de=((doctors))
OR (de=((pharmacy)))
OR Explode ((de=((health professionals)
OR (de=((medicine)))
OR (de=((medical students)))
OR (ab=(social work*))
OR (ti=(social work*))
OR (ab=(nurse or nursing or nurses))

OR (ti=(nurse or nursing or nurses))

OR (ti=(health visitor*))

OR (ab=(health visitor*))

OR (ab=(midwif* or midwive*))

OR (ti=(midwif* or midwive*))

OR (ab=(pharmacy or pharmacist*))

OR (ti=(pharmacy or pharmacist*))

OR (ab=(health care or healthcare))

OR (ti=(health care or healthcare))

OR (ab=(health profession* or health practitioner*))

OR (ti=(health profession* or health practitioner*))

OR (ab=(medical or medic or medics or clinical))

OR (ti=(medical or medic or medics or clinical))

OR ((ti=(doctor* or gp or gps or general practitioner* or family practitioner* or primary care practitioner* or physician*))

OR ((ab=(doctor* or gp or gps or general practitioner* or family practitioner* or primary care practitioner* or physician*))

****

CareData
Strategy developed by CRD and undertaken by SCIE using the inhouse version of CareData
Date 3.4.03

1. Keyword – Communication
2. Keyword – Counselling
3. Keyword – Empathy
4. (Communicat* w3 skill*) in ti,ab
5. (Communicat* w3 competen*) in ti,ab
6. (Communicat* w3 improve*) in ti,ab
7. (Communicat* w3 improving) in ti,ab
8. (Communicat* w3 enhanc*) in ti,ab
9. (Communicat* w3 develop*) in ti,ab
10. (effective* w3 Communicat*) in ti,ab
11. cst in ti,ab
12. (interpersonal w3 skill*) in ti,ab
13. (interpersonal w3 communicat*) in ti,ab

14. (consultation w3 skill*) in ti,ab
15. (consulting w3 skill*) in ti,ab
16. ((counselling or counseling) w3 skill*) in ti,ab
17. (listen* w3 skill*) in ti,ab
18. (listen* w3 develop*) in ti,ab
19. (empath* w3 communicat*) in ti,ab
20. (empath* w3 skill*) in ti,ab
21. or/1-20
22. Keywords - teaching methods
23. Keyword - practice teaching
24. Keyword – national vocational qualifications
25. Keyword – post qualifying education
26. Keyword – practice teachers
27. Keyword - diploma in social work
28. Keyword – training
29. Keyword – evaluation
30. Keyword - social work education
31. (training or trained or trainer* or train) in ti,ab
32. (course* or workshop* or work-shop* or programme* or program or programs) in ti,ab
33. (educat* or pedagog*) in ti,ab
34. (teach* or taught or instruction* or tuition* or supervise*) in ti,ab
35. (tutor* or facilitat*) in ti,ab
36. (Learn* or curriculum or curricula) in ti,ab
37. (classes or lecture* or seminar) in ti,ab
38. or/22-38
39. 21 and 38
40. keyword student social workers
41. keyword - social workers
42. key word - general practitioners
43. keyword - medical staff
44. keyword - health visitors
45. social work* in ti,ab
46. (nurse or nurses or nursing) in ti,ab
47. (health visitor*) in ti,ab
48. (midwife*/midwive*) in ti,ab
49. (pharmacy/pharmacist*) in ti,ab
50. (health care/healthcare) in ti,ab
51. (health professional*/health practitioner*) in ti,ab

52. (medical or medic or medics or clinical) in ti,ab
53. (doctor/gp/gps/general practitioner*/family practitioner*/primary care practitioner*/physician*) in ti,ab
54. or/40-53
55. 39 and 54

****

SIGLE 1982-2002/12 (ARC Silverplatter)
Searched 12.3.03

#1 (communicat* near3 skill*)
#2 (communicat* near3 competen*)
#3 (communicat* near3 improve*)
#4 (communicat* near3 improving)
#5 (communicat* near3 enhanc*)
#6 (communicat* near3 develop*)
#7 (effective* near3 communicat*)
#8 cst
#9 (interpersonal near3 skill*)
#10 (interpersonal near3 communicat*)
#11 (consultation* near3 skill*)
#12 (consulting near3 skill*)
#13 counsel?ing near3 skill*
#14 (listen* near3 skill*)
#15 (listen* near3 develop*)
#16 (empath* near3 communicat*)
#17 (interprofession* near3 communicat*)
#18 (empath* near3 skill*)
#19 #1 or #2 or #3 or #4 or #5 or #6 or #7 or #8 or #9 or #10 or #11 or #12 or #13 or #14 or #15 or #16 or #17 or #18
#20 training or trained or trainer* or train
#21 course* or workshop* or work-shop* or program or programs or programme*
#22 (educat* or pedagog*)
#23 teach* or taught or instruction* or tuition* or supervis*
#24 tutor* or facilitat*
#25 learn* or curriculum or curricula*

#26 classes or lecture* or seminar*

#27 #20 or #21 or #22 or #23 or #24 or #25 or #26

#28 #19 and #27

#29 social work*

#30 nurse or nurses or nursing

#31 health visitor*

#32 midwif* or midwive*

#33 pharmacy or pharmacist*

#34 health professional* or health practitioner*

#35 medical or medic or medics or clinical

#36 (doctor* or gp or gps or general practitoner* or family practitoner* or primary care practitoner* or physician*)

#37 #29 or #30 or #31 or #32 or #33 or #34 or #35 or #36

#38 #28 and #37

#39 #38 and (PY = 1982-2002)

****

Dissertation Abstracts Online (file 35)
Social SciSearch (File 7)
Wilson Social Sciences Abstracts (file 142)

These databases were searched together using the DIALOG service on 13.3.03.

The strategy was confined to social work due to the high cost of printing the large number of hits generated by the original broader strategy.

B 35,7,142

s (communication or communicate or communicates or communicating or communicated)(3w)(skill or skills or skilled or skilling))/ti,ab

s ((communication or communicate or communicates or communicating or communicated)(3w)competen?)/ti,ab

s ((communication or communicate or communicates or communicating or communicated)(3w)(improve or improves or improving or improved))/ti,ab

s ((communication or communicate or communicates or communicating or communicated)(3w)(enhance or enhances or enhancing or enhanced))/ti,ab s   ((communication or communicate or communicates or communicating or communicated)(3w)(develop or develops or developing or developed))/ti,ab

s   (effective?(3w)(communication or communicate or communicates or communicating or communicated))/ti,ab

s   (interpersonal(3w)(skill or skills or skilled or skilling))/ti,ab

s   (interpersonal(3w)(communication or communicate or communicates or communicating or communicated))/ti,ab

s   (consultation?(3w)(skill or skills or skilling or skilled))/ti,ab

s   (consulting(3w)(skill or skills or skilling or skilled))/ti,ab

s   (counseling(3w)(skill or skills or skilling or skilled))/ti,ab

s   (counselling(3w)(skill or skills or skilling or skilled))/ti,ab

s   (listen?(3w)(skill or skills or skilling or skilled))/ti,ab

s   (listen?(3w)(develop or develops or developing or developed))/ti,ab

s   (empath?(3w)(communication or communicate or communicates or communicating or communicated))/ti,ab

s   (empath?(3w)(skill or skills or skilling or skilled?))/ti,ab

s   (interprofession?(3w)(communication or communicate or communicates or communicating or communicated))/ti,ab

s   s1 or s2 or s3 or s4 or s5 or s6 or s7 or s8 or s9 or s10 or s11 or s12 or s13 or s14 or s15 or s16 or s17

s   (training or trained or trainer? or train)/ti,ab

s   (course or courses or workshop? or work-shop? or program or programs or programme?)/ti,ab

s   (education or educate or educates or educating or educated or pedagog?)/ti,ab

s   (teach or teaches or teaching or taught or instruction? or tuition or supervise or supervision)/ti,ab

s   (tutor or tutors or tutorial? or facilitate? or facilitating or facilitator? or supervisor?)/ti,ab

s   (learn or learns or learning or learnt or curriculum or curricula?)/ti,ab

s (lecture? or seminar? or classes)/ti,ab

s   s19 or s20 or s21 or s22 or s23 or s24 or s25

s   (social(w)work or social(w)worker?)/ti,ab

s   s18 and s26 and s27

s   s28 and PY=1982:2003

RD s29

IBSS (International Bibliography of Social Sciences) 1982–2003/3 (BIDS) bidsibss@mu.ingenta.com
Searched 13.3.03

(communicat★ skill★ or skill★ communicat★ or communicat★ competen★ or
    competen★ communicat★ or communicat★ improv★ or improv★ communicat★
    or communicat★ enhanc★ or enhanc★ communicat★ or communicat★ develop★
    or develop★ communicat★ or effective★ communicat★ or communicat★
    effective★ or cst) @TKA
(interpersonal skill★ or interpersonal communicat★ or consultation skill★ or
    consulting skill★)@TKA
(counselling skill★ or skill★ counselling or counseling skill★ or skill★
    counseling)@TKA
(listen★ skill★ or skill★ listen★ or listen★ develop★ or develop★ listen★)@TKA
(empath★ communicat★ or communicat★ empath★ or empath★ skill★ or skill★
    empath★ or interprofession★ communicat★)@TKA

★★

ERIC 1982–2002/12 (Silverplatter CDROM)
Searched 17.3.02

#1   "Interpersonal-Communication" in DEM,DER
#2   communication skills in DEM,DER
#3   nonverbal communication in DEM,DER
#4   empathy in DEM,DER
#5   listening skills in DEM,DER
#6   counseling techniques in DEM,DER
#7   (communicat★ near3 competen★) in ti,ab
#8   (communicat★ near3 skill★) in ti,ab
#9   (communicat★ near3 improve★) in ti,ab
#10   (communicat★ near3 improving★) in ti,ab
#11   (communicat★ near3 enhanc★) in ti,ab
#12   (communicat★ near3 develop★) in ti,ab
#13   (effective★ near3 communicat★) in ti,ab
#14   cst in ti,ab
#15   (interpersonal near3 skill★) in ti,ab
#16   (interpersonal near3 communicat★) in ti,ab
#17   (consultation★ near3 skill★) in ti,ab

#18 (consulting near3 skill*) in ti,ab

#19 (counsel?ing near3 skill*) in ti,ab

#20 (listen* near3 skill*) in ti,ab

#21 (listen* near3 develop*) in ti,ab

#22 (empath* near3 communicat*) in ti,ab

#23 (empath* near3 skill*) in ti,ab

#24 (interprofession* near3 communicat*) in ti,ab

#25 #1 or #2 or #3 or #4 or #5 or #6 or #7 or #8 or #9 or #10 or #11 or #12 or #13 or #14 or #15 or #16 or #17 or #18 or #19 or #20 or #21 or #22 or #23 or #24

#26 interpersonal competence in DEM,DER

#27 competency based education in DEM,DER

#28 competency based teacher education in DEM,DER

#29 course evaluation in DEM,DER

#30 curriculum evaluation in DEM,DER

#31 curriculum development in DEM,DER

#32 teaching methods in DEM,DER

#33 teaching styles in DEM,DER

#34 student evaluation in DEM,DER

#35 teacher evaluation in DEM,DER

#36 program effectiveness in DEM,DER

#37 professional training in DEM,DER

#38 professional education in DEM,DER

#39 vocational education in DEM,DER

#40 allied health occupations education in DEM,DER

#41 medical education in DEM,DER

#42 graduate medical education in DEM,DER

#43 nursing education in DEM,DER

#44 (training or trained or trainer* or train) in ti, ab

#45 (course* or workshop* or work-shop$ or program or programs or programme*) in ti, ab

#46 (teach* or taught or instruction* or tuition* or supervis*) in ti,ab

#47 (tutor* or facilitat*) in ti,ab

#48 (learn* or curriculum or curricula) in ti,ab

#49 (classes or lecture* or seminar*) in ti,ab

#50 #26 or #27 or #28 or #29 or #30 or #31 or #32 or #33 or #34 or #35 or #36 or #37 or #38 or #39 or #40 or #41 or #42 or #43 or #44 or #45 or #46 or #47 or #48 or #49

#51 #25 and #50

#52 social work in DEM,DER

#53 social workers in DEM,DER

#54 pharmacy in DEM,DER

#55 pharmacists in DEM,DER

#56 nurses in DEM,DER

#57 health personnel in DEM,DER

#58 medical schools in DEM,DER

#59 medical students in DEM,DER

#60 physicians in DEM,DER

#61 (social work*) in ti,ab

#62 (nurse or nurses or nursing) in ti,ab

#63 (health visitor*) in ti,ab

#64 (midwif* or midwive*) in ti,ab

#65 (pharmacy or pharmacist*) in ti,ab

#66 (health care or healthcare) in ti,ab

#67 (health professional* or health practitioner*) in ti,ab

#68 (medical or medic or medics or clinical) in ti,ab

#69 (doctor* or gp or gps or general practitioner* or family practitioner* or primary care practitioner* or physician*) in ti,ab

#70 #52 or #53 or #54 or #55 or #56 or #57 or #58 or #59 or #59 or #60 or #61 or #62 or #63 or #64 or #65 or #66 or #67 or #68 or #69

#71 #51 and #70

****

British Education Index 1986-2002/11 (BIDS OVID)
Searched 17.3.03

1   communication skills/

2   Nonverbal communication/

3   Interpersonal communication/

4   Empathy/

5   Counselling techniques/

6   Listening skills/

7   (communicat$ adj3 skill$).ti, ab.

8   (communicat$ adj3 competen$).ti, ab.

9   (communicat$ adj3 improve$).ti, ab.

10   (communicat$ adj3 improving$).ti, ab.

11   (communicat$ adj3 enhanc$).ti, ab.

12   (communicat$ adj3 develop$).ti, ab.

13   (effective$ adj3 communicat$).ti, ab.

14   cst.ti, ab.

15   (interpersonal adj3 skill$).ti, ab.

16   (interpersonal adj3 communicat$).ti, ab.

17   (consultation$ adj3 skill$).ti, ab.

18   (consulting adj3 skill$).ti, ab.

19   (counsel?ing adj3 skill$).ti, ab.

20   (listen$ adj3 skill$).ti, ab.

21   (listen$ adj3 develop$).ti, ab.

22   (empath$ adj3 communicat$).ti, ab.

23   (empath$ adj3 skill$).ti, ab.

24   (interprofession$ adj3 communicat$).ti, ab.

25   or/1-24

26   Competency based education/

27   Competency based teacher education/

28   Interpersonal competence/

29   Course evaluation/

30   Curriculum evaluation/

31   curriculum development/

32   teacher evaluation/

33   student evaluation/

34   teaching methods/

35   teaching styles/

36   professional training/

37   professional education/

38   vocational education/

39   allied health occupations education/

40   medical education/

41   nursing education/

42   (training or trained or trainer$ or train).ti, ab.

43   (course$ or workshop$ or work-shop$ or program or programs or programme$).ti, ab.

44   (teach$ or taught or instruction$ or tuition$ or supervis$).ti, ab.

45   (tutor$ or facilitat$).ti, ab.

46   (learn$ or curriculum or curricula).ti, ab.

47   (classes or lecture$ or seminar$).ti, ab.

48   or/26-47

49   25 and 48

50   social workers/

51   social work/

52   pharmacy/

53   pharmacists/

54   nurses/

55   Nursing/

56   health personnel/

57   medical schools/

58   medical students/

59   physicians/

60   social work$.ti, ab.

61   (nurse or nurses or nursing).ti, ab.

62   health visitor$.ti, ab.

63   (midwif$ or midwive$).ti, ab.

64   (pharmacy or pharmacist).ti, ab.

65   (healthcare or health care).ti, ab.

66   (health profession$ or health practitioner$).ti, ab.

67   (medical or medic or medics or clinical).ti, ab.

78   doctor$ or gp or gps or general practitioner$ or family practitioner$ or
      primary care practitioner$ or physician$).ti, ab.

79   or/50-78

72   49 and 79

****

PsycINFO 1982–2003/3 week 2 (Silverplatter CD Rom) Searched 19.3.03

#1   "Communication-Skills-Training" in DE

#2   "communication-skills" in DE

#3   "interpersonal-communication" in DE

#4   "nonverbal-communication" in DE

#5   «empathy» in DE

#6   "Listening-Interpersonal" in DE

#7   (communicat* near3 skill*) in ti,ab

#8   (communicat* near3 competen*) in ti,ab

#9   (communicat* near3 improve*) in ti,ab

#10   (communicat* near3 improving) in ti,ab

#11   (communicat* near3 enhanc*) in ti,ab

#12 (communicat* near3 develop*) in ti,ab

#13 (effective* near3 communicat*) in ti,ab

#14 cst in ti,ab

#15 (interpersonal near3 skill*) in ti,ab

#16 (interpersonal near3 communicat*) in ti,ab

#17 (consultation* near3 skill*) in ti,ab

#18 (consulting near3 skill*) in ti,ab

#19 (counsel?ing near3 skill*) in ti,ab

#20 (listen* near3 skill*) in ti,ab

#21 (listen* near3 develop*) in ti,ab

#22 (empath* near3 communicat*) in ti,ab

#23 (empath* near3 skill*) in ti,ab

#24 (interprofession* near3 communicat*) in ti,ab

#25 #1 or #2 or #3 or #4 or #5 or #6 or #7 or #8 or #9 or #10 or #11 or #12 or #13 or #14 or #15 or #16 or #17 or #18 or #19 or #20 or #21 or #22 or #23 or #24

#26 "course-evaluation" in DE

#27 "curriculum-development" in DE

#28 "teaching-methods" in DE

#29 "educational-program-evaluation" in DE

#30 "teacher-effectiveness-evaluation" in DE

#31 "vocational-education" in DE

#32 "higher-education" in DE

#33 "undergraduate-education" in DE

#34 "graduate-education" in DE

#35 "medical-education" in de

#36 "nursing-education" in DE

#37 "social-work-education" in de

#38 (training or trained or trainer* or train) in ti,ab

#39 (course* or workshop* or work-shop*) in ti,ab

#40 (program or programs or programme*) in ti,ab

#41 (educat* or pedagog*) in ti,ab

#42 (teach* or taught or instruction* or tuition* or supervis*) in ti,ab

#43 (tutor* or facilitat*) in ti,ab

#44 (learn* or curriculum or curricula) in ti,ab

#45 (classes or lecture* or seminar*) in ti,ab

#46 #26 or #27 or #28 or #29 or #30 or #31 or #32 or #33 or #34 or #35 or #36 or #37 or #38 or #39 or #40 or #41 or #42 or #43 or #44 or #45

#47 explode "Medical-Personnel" in DE
#48 "nursing-students" in de
#49 "medical-students" in DE
#50 "social-workers" in de
#51 "midwifery" in de
#52 (social work*) in ti,ab
#53 (nurse or nurses or nursing) in ti,ab
#54 (health visitor*) in ti,ab
#55 (midwif* or midwive*) in ti,ab
#56 (pharmacy or pharmacist*) in ti,ab
#57 (health care or healthcare) in ti,ab
#58 (health professional* or health practitioner*) in ti,ab
#59 (medical or medic or medics or clinical) in ti,ab
#60 (doctor or gp or gps or general practitioner* or family practitioner* or primary care practitioner* or physician*)in ti,ab
#61 #47 or #48 or #49 or #50 or #51 or #52 or #53 or #54 or #55 or #56 or #57 or #58 or #59 or #60
#62 #25 and #46
#63 #62 and #61

****

HMIC 1982-2003 (ARC Silverplatter)
Searched 19.3.03

#1   "communication-skills" in DE
#2   "interpersonal-communication" in DE
#3   "interpersonal-skills" in DE
#4   "empathy" in DE
#5   "counselling-skills" in DE
#6   (communicat* near3 skill*) in ti,ab
#7   (communicat* near3 competen*) in ti,ab
#8   (communicat* near3 improve*) in ti,ab
#9   (communicat* near3 improving) in ti,ab
#10 (communicat* near3 enhanc*) in ti,ab
#11 (communicat* near3 develop*) in ti,ab
#12 (effective* near3 communicat*) in ti,ab
#13 cst in ti,ab
#14 (interpersonal near3 skill*) in ti,ab

#15   (interpersonal near3 communicat*) in ti,ab
#16   (consultation* near3 skill*) in ti,ab
#17   (consulting near3 skill*) in ti,ab
#18   (counsel?ing near3 skill*) in ti,ab
#19   (listen* near3 skill*) in ti,ab
#20   (listen* near3 develop*) in ti,ab
#21   (empath* near3 communicat*) in ti,ab
#22   (empath* near3 skill*) in ti,ab
#23   (interprofession* near3 communicat*) in ti,ab
#24   #1 or #2 or #3 or #4 or #5 or #6 or #7 or #8 or #9 or #10 or #11 or #12 or #13 or #14 or #15 or #16 or #17 or #18 or #19 or #20 or #21 or #22 or #23
#25   "educational assessment" in de
#26   "curriculum-development" in de
#27   "teaching-methods" in de
#28   "vocational-training" in de
#29   "professional-education" in de
#30   "professional-competence"
#31   "higher-education" in de
#32   "nursing-education" in de
#33   "medical-education" in de
#34   "undergraduate-education" in DE
#35   "undergraduate-medical-education" in de
#36   "social-worker-qualifications" in de
#37   "social-worker-professional-qualifications" in de
#38   "social-worker-training" in de
#39   ((training or trained or trainer* or train) near4 (effectiv* or efficac* or competenc* or evaluat* or assess* or measur* or analysis or analys* or analyz* or apprais*)) in ti,ab
#40   ((course* or workshop* or work-shop*) near4 (effectiv* or efficac* or competenc* or evaluat* or assess* or measur* or analysis or analys* or analyz* or apprais*)) in ti,ab
#41   ((program or programs or programme*) near4 (effectiv* or efficac* or competenc* or evaluat* or assess* or measur* or analysis or analys* or analyz* or apprais*)) in ti,ab
#42   ((educat* or pedagog*) near4 (effectiv* or efficac* or competenc* or evaluat* or assess* or measur* or analysis or analys* or analyz* or apprais*)) in ti,ab

#43 ((teach* or taught or instruction* or tuition* or supervis*) near4 (effectiv* or efficac* or competenc* or evaluat* or assess* or measur* or analysis or analys* or analyz* or apprais*)) in ti,ab

#44 ((tutor* or facilitat*) near4 (effectiv* or efficac* or competenc* or evaluat* or assess* or measur* or analysis or analys* or analyz* or apprais*)) in ti,ab

#45 ((learn* or curriculum or curricula) near4 (effectiv* or efficac* or competenc* or evaluat* or assess* or measur* or analysis or analys* or analyz* or apprais*)) in ti,ab

#46 (student* near4 (competenc* or evaluat* or assess* or apprais*)) in ti,ab

#47 ((training or skills or instruction* or teaching) near4 (program* or programme* or course* or workshop* or work-shop* or technique*)) in ti,ab

#48 (skills near4 (teaching or training or competenc*)) in ti,ab

#49 ((pedagog* or educat*) near4 training) in ti,ab

#50 #25 or #26 or #27 or #28 or #29 or #30 or #31 or #32 or #33 or #34 or #35 or #36 or #37 or #38 or #39 or #40 or #41 or #42 or #43 or #44 or #45 or #46 or #47 or #48 or #49

#51 #24 and #50

#52 #51 and (PY = 1982-2003)

****

British Nursing Index (BNI) 1994 to March 2003 (Ovid Web) Searched 19.3.03

1   communication/
2   (communicat$ adj3 skill$).ti,ab.
3   (communicat$ adj3 competen$).ti,ab.
4   (communicat$ adj3 improve$).ti,ab.
5   (communicat$ adj3 improving).ti,ab.
6   (communicat$ adj3 enhanc$).ti,ab.
7   (communicat$ adj3 develop$).ti,ab.
8   (effective$ adj3 communicat$).ti,ab.
9   (communicat$ adj3 training).ti,ab.
10   (communicat$ adj3 teach$).ti,ab.
11   (communicat$ adj3 taught).ti,ab.
12   (communicat$ adj3 technique$).ti,ab.
13   cst.ti,ab.
14   (interpersonal adj3 skill$).ti,ab.

15   (interpersonal adj3 communicat$).ti,ab.

16   (consultation$ adj3 skill$).ti,ab.

17   (consulting adj3 skill$).ti,ab.

18   (counsel?ng adj3 skill$).ti,ab.

19   (listen$ adj3 skill$).ti,ab.

20   (listen$ adj3 develop$).ti,ab.

21   (empath$ adj3 communicat$).ti,ab.

22   (empath$ adj3 skill$).ti,ab.

23   (interprofession$ adj3 communicat$).ti,ab.

24   or/1-23

25   education assessment/

26   education course evaluation/

27   professional development/

28   ((training or trained or trainer$ or train) adj4 (effectiv$ or efficac$ or
      competenc$ or evaluat$ or assess$ or measur$ or analysis$ or analys$ or
      analyz$ or apprais$)).ti,ab.

29   ((course$ or workshop$ or work-shop or program or programs or
      programme$) adj4 (effectiv$ or efficac$ or competenc$ or evaluat$ or assess$
      or measur$ or analysis$ or analys$ or analyz$ or apprais$)).ti,ab.

30   ((teach$ or taught or instruction$ or tuition$ or tutor$) adj4 (effectiv$ or
      efficac$ or competenc$ or evaluat$ or assess$ or measur$ or analysis$ or
      analys$ or analyz$ or apprais$)).ti,ab.

31   ((pedagog$ or educat$) adj4 (effectiv$ or efficac$ or competenc$ or evaluat$
      or assess$ or measur$ or analysis$ or analys$ or analyz$ or apprais$)).ti,ab.

32   ((supervision or supervisor$ or facilitator$) adj4 (effectiv$ or efficac$ or
      competenc$ or evaluat$ or assess$ or measur$ or analysis$ or analys$ or
      analyz$ or apprais$)).ti,ab.

33   (learn$ adj4 (effectiv$ or efficac$ or competenc$ or evaluat$ or assess$ or
      measur$ or analysis$ or analys$ or analyz$ or apprais$)).ti,ab.

34   ((curricula or curriculum) adj4 (effectiv$ or efficac$ or competenc$ or
      evaluat$ or assess$ or measur$ or analysis$ or analys$ or analyz$ or apprais$
      or design$)).ti,ab.

35   (student$ adj4 (competenc$ or evaluat$ or assess$ or apprais$)).ti,ab.

36   ((training or skills or instruction$ or teaching) adj4 (program$ or
      programme$ or course$ or workshop$ or work-shop$ or technique$)).ti,ab.

37   (skills adj4 (teaching or training or competenc$)).ti,ab

38   ((pedagog$ or educat$) adj4 training).ti,ab.

39   or/25-38

40   24 and 39

CINAHL 1982–2003/03 (OVID web)
Searched 19.3.03

1   communication skills training/

2   exp nonverbal communication/

3   negotiating/

4   (communicat$ adj3 skill$).ti,ab.

5   (communicat$ adj3 competen$).ti,ab.

6   (communicat$ adj3 improve$).ti,ab.

7   (communicat$ adj3 improving).ti,ab.

8   (communicat$ adj3 enhanc$).ti,ab.

9   (communicat$ adj3 develop$).ti,ab.

10 (effective$ adj3 communicat$).ti,ab.

11 (communicat$ adj3 training).ti,ab.

12 (communicat$ adj3 teach$).ti,ab.

13 (communicat$ adj3 taught).ti,ab.

14 (communicat$ adj3 technique$).ti,ab.

15 cst.ti,ab.

16 (interpersonal adj3 skill$).ti,ab.

17 (interpersonal adj3 communicat$).ti,ab.

18 (consultation$ adj3 skill$).ti,ab.

19 (consulting adj3 skill$).ti,ab.

20 (counsel?ng adj3 skill$).ti,ab.

21 (listen$ adj3 skill$).ti,ab.

22 (listen$ adj3 develop$).ti,ab.

23 (empath$ adj3 communicat$).ti,ab.

24 (empath$ adj3 skill$).ti,ab.

25 (interprofession$ adj3 communicat$).ti,ab.

26 or/1-25

27 competency based education/

28 competency assessment/

29 professional competence/

30 vocational education/

31 course evaluation/

32 student performance appraisal/

33 ((training or trained or trainer$ or train) adj4 (effectiv$ or efficac$ or
     competenc$ or evaluat$ or assess$ or measur$ or analysis$ or analys$ or
     analyz$ or apprais$)).ti,ab.

34   ((course$ or workshop$ or work-shop or program or programs or
      programme$) adj4 (effectiv$ or efficac$ or competenc$ or evaluat$ or assess$
      or measur$ or analysis$ or analys$ or analyz$ or apprais$)).ti,ab.

35   ((teach$ or taught or instruction$ or tuition$ or tutor$) adj4 (effectiv$ or
      efficac$ or competenc$ or evaluat$ or assess$ or measur$ or analysis$ or
      analys$ or analyz$ or apprais$)).ti,ab.

36   ((pedagog$ or educat$) adj4 (effectiv$ or efficac$ or competenc$ or evaluat$
      or assess$ or measur$ or analysis$ or analys$ or analyz$ or apprais$)).ti,ab.

37   ((supervision or supervisor$ or facilitator$) adj4 (effectiv$ or efficac$ or
      competenc$ or evaluat$ or assess$ or measur$ or analysis$ or analys$ or
      analyz$ or apprais$)).ti,ab.

38   (learn$ adj4 (effectiv$ or efficac$ or competenc$ or evaluat$ or assess$ or
      measur$ or analysis$ or analys$ or analyz$ or apprais$)).ti,ab.

39   ((curricula or curriculum) adj4 (effectiv$ or efficac$ or competenc$ or
      evaluat$ or assess$ or measur$ or analysis$ or analys$ or analyz$ or apprais$
      or design$)).ti,ab.

40   (student$ adj4 (competenc$ or evaluat$ or assess$ or apprais$)).ti,ab.

41   ((training or skills or instruction$ or teaching) adj4 (program$ or
      programme$ or course$ or workshop$ or work-shop$ or technique$)).ti,ab.

42   (skills adj4 (teaching or training or competenc$)).ti,ab.

43   ((pedagog$ or educat$) adj4 training).ti,ab.

44   or/27-43

45   26 and 44

****

MEDLINE 1982-2003/03 (OVID Web)
Searched 19.3.03

1   persuasive communication/
2   interdisciplinary communication/
3   exp nonverbal communication/
4   negotiating/
5   (communicat$ adj3 skill$).ti,ab.
6   (communicat$ adj3 competen$).ti,ab.
7   (communicat$ adj3 improve$).ti,ab.
8   (communicat$ adj3 improving).ti,ab.
9   (communicat$ adj3 enhanc$).ti,ab.
10   (communicat$ adj3 develop$).ti,ab.

11   (effective$ adj3 communicat$).ti,ab.

12   (communicat$ adj3 training).ti,ab.

13   (communicat$ adj3 teach$).ti,ab.

14   (communicat$ adj3 taught).ti,ab.

15   (communicat$ adj3 technique$).ti,ab.

16   cst.ti,ab.

17   (interpersonal adj3 skill$).ti,ab.

18   (interpersonal adj3 communicat$).ti,ab.

19   (consultation$ adj3 skill$).ti,ab.

20   (consulting adj3 skill$).ti,ab.

21   (counsel?ng adj3 skill$).ti,ab.

22   (listen$ adj3 skill$).ti,ab.

23   (listen$ adj3 develop$).ti,ab.

24   (empath$ adj3 communicat$).ti,ab.

25   (empath$ adj3 skill$).ti,ab.

26   (interprofession$ adj3 communicat$).ti,ab.

27   or/1-26

28   competency based education/

29   professional education/

30   vocational education/

31   program evaluation/

32   inservice training/

33   ((training or trained or trainer$ or train) adj4 (effectiv$ or efficac$ or competenc$ or evaluat$ or assess$ or measur$ or analysis$ or analys$ or analyz$ or apprais$)).ti,ab.

34   ((course$ or workshop$ or work-shop or program or programs or programme$) adj4 (effectiv$ or efficac$ or competenc$ or evaluat$ or assess$ or measur$ or analysis$ or analys$ or analyz$ or apprais$)).ti,ab.

35   ((teach$ or taught or instruction$ or tuition$ or tutor$) adj4 (effectiv$ or efficac$ or competenc$ or evaluat$ or assess$ or measur$ or analysis$ or analys$ or analyz$ or apprais$)).ti,ab.

36   ((pedagog$ or educat$) adj4 (effectiv$ or efficac$ or competenc$ or evaluat$ or assess$ or measur$ or analysis$ or analys$ or analyz$ or apprais$)).ti,ab.

37   ((supervision or supervisor$ or facilitator$) adj4 (effectiv$ or efficac$ or competenc$ or evaluat$ or assess$ or measur$ or analysis$ or analys$ or analyz$ or apprais$)).ti,ab.

38   (learn$ adj4 (effectiv$ or efficac$ or competenc$ or evaluat$ or assess$ or measur$ or analysis$ or analys$ or analyz$ or apprais$)).ti,ab.

39   ((curricula or curriculum) adj4 (effectiv$ or efficac$ or competenc$ or evaluat$ or assess$ or measur$ or analysis$ or analys$ or analyz$ or apprais$ or design$)).ti,ab.
40   (student$ adj4 (competenc$ or evaluat$ or assess$ or apprais$)).ti,ab.
41   ((training or skills or instruction$ or teaching) adj4 (program$ or programme$ or course$ or workshop$ or work-shop$ or technique$)).ti,ab.
42   (skills adj4 (teaching or training or competenc$)).ti,ab.
43   ((pedagog$ or educat$) adj4 training).ti,ab.
44   or/28-43
45   27and 44

****

Cochrane Library Issue 1 2003 (Update software CD Rom) Searched 21.3.03

1   PERSUASIVE COMMUNICATION single term (MESH)
2   NONVERBAL COMMUNICATION Explode all trees (MESH)
3   NEGOTIATING single term (MESH)
4   (communicat* next skill*)
5   (skill* next communicat*)
6   ((communicat* next competen*) or (competen* next communicat*))
7   ((communicat* next improve*) or (improve* next communicat*))
8   ((communicat* next improving) or (improving next comunicat*))
9   (communicat* next enhanc*) or (enhanc* next communicat*))
10   ((communicat* next develop*) or (develop* next communicat*))
11   ((effective* next communicat*) or (communicat* next effective*))
12   ((communicat* next training) or (training next communicat*))
13   ((communicat* next teach*) or (teach* next communicat*))
14   ((communicat* next taught) or (taught next communicat*))
15   ((communicat* next technique*) or (technique* next communicat*))
16   cst
17   (interpersonal next skill*)
18   (interpersonal next communicat*)
19   ((consultation* next skill*) or (skill* next consultation*))
20   ((consulting next skill*) or (skill* next consulting))
21   ((listen* next skill*) or (listen* next skill*))
22   (develop* next listen*)
23   (listen* next develop*)

24   ((empath* next communicat*) or (communicat* next empath*))
25   ((empath* next skill*) or (skill* next empath*))
26   (interprofession* next communicat*)
27   (#1 or #2 or #3 or #4 or #5 or #6 or #7 or #8 or #9 or #10 or #11 or
     #12 or #13 or #14 or #15 or #16 or #17 or #18 or #19 or #20 or #21
     or #22 or #23 or #24 or #25 or #26)
28   COMPETENCY-BASED EDUCATION single term (MESH)
29   EDUCATION PROFESSIONAL single term (MESH)
30   VOCATIONAL EDUCATION single term (MESH)
31   PROGRAM EVALUATION single term (MESH
32   INSERVICE TRAINING single term (MESH)
33   ((train* near effective*) or (train* near efficac*) or (train* near competenc*)
     or (train near evaluat*) or (train* near assess*) or (train* near measure*) or
     (train* near analysis) or (train* near analys*) or (train* near analyz*) or
     (train* near apprais*))
34   ((course* near effective*) or (course* near efficac*) or (course* near
     competenc*) or (course* near evaluat*) or (course* near assess*) or
     (course* near measure*) or (course* near analysis) or (course* near analys*)
     or (course* near analyz*) or (course* near apprais*))
35   ((workshop* near effective*) or (workshop* near efficac*) or (workshop*
     near competenc*) or (workshop* near evaluat*) or (workshop* near
     assess*) or (workshop* near measure*) or (workshop* near analysis) or
     (workshop* near analys*) or (workshop* near analyz*) or (workshop* near
     apprais*))
36   ((work-shop* near effective*) or (work-shop* near efficac*) or (work-
     shop* near competenc*) or (work-shop* near evaluat*) or (work-shop*
     near assess*) or (work-shop* near measure*) or (work-shop* near analysis)
     or (work-shop* near analys*) or (work-shop* near analyz*) or (work-
     shop* near apprais*))
37   ((program* near effective*) or (program* near efficac*) or (program* near
     competenc*) or (program* near evaluat*) or (program* near assess*) or
     (program* near measure*) or (program* near analysis) or (program* near
     analys*) or (program* near analyz*) or (program* near apprais*))
38   ((teach* near effective*) or (teach* near efficac*) or (teach* near
     competenc*) or (teach* near evaluat*) or (teach* near assess*) or (teach*
     near measure*) or (teach* near analysis) or (teach* near analys*) or (teach*
     near analyz*) or (teach* near apprais*))
39   ((taught near effective*) or (taught near efficac*) or (taught near
     competenc*) or (taught near evaluat*) or (taught near assess*) or (taught

near measure*) or (taught near analysis) or (taught near analys*) or (taught near analyz*) or (taught near apprais*))

40   ((instruction* near effective*) or (instruction* near efficac*) or (instruction* near competenc*) or (instruction* near evaluat*) or (instruction* near assess*) or (instruction* near measure*) or (instruction* near analysis) or (instruction* near analys*) or (instruction* near analyz*) or (instruction* near apprais*))

41   ((tuition* near effective*) or (tuition* near efficac*) or (tuition* near competenc*) or (tuition* near evaluat*) or (tuition* near assess*) or (tuition* near measure*) or (tuition* near analysis) or (tuition* near analys*) or (tuition* near analyz*) or (tuition* near apprais*))

42   ((tutor* near effective*) or (tutor* near efficac*) or (tutor* near competenc*) or (tutor* near evaluat*) or (tutor* near assess*) or (tutor* near measure*) or (tutor* near analysis) or (tutor* near analys*) or (tutor* near analyz*) or (tutor* near apprais*))

43   ((pedagog* near effective*) or (pedagog* near efficac*) or (pedagog* near competenc*) or (pedagog* near evaluat*) or (pedagog* near assess*) or (pedagog* near measure*) or (pedagog* near analysis) or (pedagog* near analys*) or (pedagog* near analyz*) or (pedagog* near apprais*))

44   ((educat* near effective*) or (educat* near efficac*) or (educat* near competenc*) or (educat* near evaluat*) or (educat* near assess*) or (educat* near measure*) or (educat* near analysis) or (educat* near analys*) or (educat* near analyz*) or (educat* near apprais*))

45   ((supervisio* near effective*) or (supervisio* near efficac*) or (supervisio* near competenc*) or (supervisio* near evaluat*) or (supervisio* near assess*) or (supervisio* near measure*) or (supervisio* near analysis) or (supervisio* near analys*) or (supervisio* near analyz*) or (supervisio* near apprais*))

46   ((facilitat* near effective*) or (facilitat* near efficac*) or (facilitat* near competenc*) or (facilitat* near evaluat*) or (facilitat* near assess*) or (facilitat* near measure*) or (facilitat* near analysis) or (facilitat* near analys*) or (facilitat* near analyz*) or (facilitat* near apprais*))

47   ((learn* near effective*) or (learn* near efficac*) or (learn* near competenc*) or (learn* near evaluat*) or (learn* near assess*) or (learn* near measure*) or (learn* near analysis) or (learn* near analys*) or (learn* near analyz*) or (learn* near apprais*))

48   ((curricul* near effective*) or (curricul* near efficac*) or (curricul* near competenc*) or (curricul* near evaluat*) or (curricul* near assess*) or (curricul* near measure*) or (curricul* near analysis) or (curricul* near

analys*) or (curricul* near analyz*) or (curricul* near apprais*) or (curricul* near design*))
49 ((student* next competenc*) or (student* next evaluat*) or (student* near assess*) or (student near apprais*))
50 ((training next program*) or (training next course) or (training next workshop) or (training next work-shop) or (training next technique*))
51 ((skills* next program*) or (skills* next course) or (skills* next workshop) or (skills* next work-shop) or (skills* next technique*))
52 ((instruction* next program*) or (instruction* next course) or (instruction* next workshop) or (instruction* next work-shop) or (instruction* next technique*))
53 ((teaching next program*) or (teaching next course) or (teaching next workshop) or (teaching next work-shop) or (teaching next technique*))
54 ((skills next teaching) or (skills next training) or (skills next competenc*))
55 ((pedagog* next training) or (educat* next training))
56 (#28 or #29 or #30 or #31 or #33 or #34 or #35 or #36 or #37 or #38 or #39 or #40 or #41 or #42 or #43 or #44 or #45 or #46 or #47 or #48 or #49 or #50 or #51 or #52 or #53 or #54 or #55)
57 (#27 and #56)

FORM 1	
1. Reviewer no 1	
2. Reviewer no 2	
3. Bibliographic details	
4. Record number (where appropriate)	

5. Please indicate the source this reference was identified from	
	Electronic database:
	Personal communication:
	Systematic hand searching:
	Internet searching:
	Personal library:
	Other:
	If OTHER please give details

5a. On initial reading of the abstract/summary is this relevant to the research review?	
	Yes
	No
	If NO to 5a please give details why NOT relevant
	If, NO, you do not need to complete 5b.

5b. If YES please indicate preliminary coding to be allocated to this abstract/record, and where applicable, to whom record should be sent.

	PT	BM	SR	LL	OM	GR
Theoretical						
Narrative						
Evaluative						
Specialised						

FORM 2					
1. Reviewer no 1					
2. Reviewer no 2					
3. Bibliographic details					
4. Record number (if applicable)					
5. Recoding/further coding (if applicable)	Theoretical	Narrative	Evaluative	Specialised	N/A
• 1st level					
• 2nd level					
• 3rd level					
• 4th level					
6. Aim of study					
7. Research					
a. Type					
b. Sample					
c. Methods					
d. Student participation	Yes No				
e. User participation	Yes No				
	If yes to d or e, details				
f. Ethics					
8. Key findings/ messages	Please give details				
9. Relevance of research to learning and teaching of qualifying social work programmes	Please give details				
10. Application – is this do-able/feasible?	Please give details				
11. Overall strengths and weaknesses/ appropriateness of methods employed	Please give details				

Annotated bibliography of key references

Paper: Collins, D. and Bogo, M. (1986) 'Competency-based field instruction: bridging the gap between laboratory and field learning', *The Clinical Supervisor*, vol 4, no 3 pp 39-52[24]

Country: Canada

Overview: Investigates the transferability of laboratory-based learning of basic interview skills into practice. 54 Masters of Social Work students were assessed before and after training and subsequently on field placement, through the assessment of taped interviews with service users. At each stage, their performance was rated on the basis of their communication of empathy, warmth and genuineness. The findings suggest that the skills observed at the end of training were not transferred to the field. The authors highlight important differences, in the specificity of objectives, in focus, and in feedback and evaluation between laboratory and field settings as student learning environments. They recommend a more systematic competency-based approach to the assessment and development of skills in the field.

* *

Text/Book: Collins, J. and Collins, M. (1992) *Social work skills training and the professional helper*, Chichester: Wiley[26]

Country: UK

Overview: This book, which acknowledges the multi-faceted and complex nature of interpersonal skills in social work practice, is divided into two halves. The first half identifies the core interpersonal skills required by social work professionals. The range of skills addressed is divided into three broad groupings: counselling skills, social work process skills (assessment, monitoring, evaluation) and social work skills in specific contexts. The book emphasises the importance of practitioners identifying their own needs with regard to interpersonal skills training through the processes of assessment, feedback and evaluation, and details how, particularly through direct observation, simulated exercises and audio/ video recording, these skills can be developed. The second addresses how practitioners can help service users develop their own interpersonal skills, and makes an important contribution to current thinking about service user involvement in social work education and the importance of developing the communication skills of service users with professionals.

****

Text/Book: Cournoyer, B. (2000) *The social work skills workbook* (3rd edn), Pacific Grove, CA: Brooks/Cole[28]
Country: USA
Overview: This workbook gives an account of 56 basic or generalist skills, that is, those skills that are common to social work practice in all, or most, settings. It also looks at the 'essential facilitative qualities' and 'professional integrity' required of social work practitioners. Using case examples, it describes a range of exercises designed to develop students' skills in interpersonal communication. For example, practitioners can evaluate their capacity for critical thinking using a 15-point *Critical Thinking Questionnaire*, or measure their capacity to accept others using a 20-point *Acceptance of Others Scale*. The third edition of this text focuses on a strengths perspective, as opposed to a more problem-oriented approach. Like other texts from North America, some themes explored in this text do not translate easily to a UK context and there is little reference to UK texts or scholarship in this field.

****

Paper: Dickson, D. and Bamford, D. (1995) 'Improving the inter-personal skills of social work students: the problem of transfer of learning and what to do about it', *British Journal of Social Work*, vol 25, no 1, pp 85-105[30]
Country: UK
Overview: This paper acknowledges the centrality of interpersonal skills for effective social work practice and the absence of a systematic overview of the state of social skills education. In particular, it focuses on the effectiveness of structured training on interview performance. The paper raises important questions about whether skills learnt in the academy are transferable to the practice context. It also provides a helpful review

of the methodological weaknesses in the limited evaluative literature on social work-based communication skills training.

****

Paper: Hansen F., Resnick, H. and Galea, J. (2002) 'Better listening: paraphrasing and perception checking – a study of the effectiveness of a multimedia skills training program', *Journal of Technology in Human Services*, vol 20, no 3/4, pp 317-31[48]
Country: Canada
Overview: This paper explores the use of multi-media and CD Rom materials, which enable students to work at their own pace in a self-directed program. Pre-test and post-tests surveys reveal that social work students found this program generally helpful, although novice students found it to be only partially effective. The context and content of the material is not easily translatable into a UK setting, however.

****

Text/Book: Hargie, O.D.W. (ed) (1997) *The handbook of communication skills* (2nd edn), London: Routledge[50]
Country: UK
Overview: This text, edited by Owen Hargie, is one of the most important and scholarly general texts in the field of communication theory. The themes covered in Part I include two background chapters by Hargie on 'Communication as skilled 'performance', and 'Interpersonal communication: a theoretical framework'. Part II looks at core communication skills, and includes chapters on the importance of non-verbal behaviour, questioning, reinforcement, reflecting, explaining, self-disclosure, listening, humour and laughter. Part III looks at more specialised contexts, Part IV at interviewing and Part V at training. This last section is particularly important in relation to the teaching and learning of communication skills. In places, the text draws heavily on cognitive and behavioural theories and this perspective, and some of the terminology used, may not find favour for those who find this language too mechanistic.

Book chapter: Jessup, H. and Rogerson, S. (1999) 'Postmodernism and the teaching and practice of interpersonal skills', in J. Pease and J. Fook (eds) *Social work practice: Postmodern critical perspectives*, London: Routledge[54]
Country: Australia
Overview: The authors acknowledge that social work has "long borrowed the tools of other disciplines" [243], but argue that social work is a separate discipline that "requires a specific form of interpersonal communication"[243]. That is, it needs to develop its own form of interpersonal communication that "links the interface between the personal and sociostructural" [243]. The paper goes on to provide an account of a postmodern and poststructuralist approach to the task of teaching and learning social work skills, highlighting the different teaching skills and strategies used in this approach. Although the paper attempts to define many of the terms used (dichotomy, postmodern, poststructural, discourse analysis), and to apply these theories in practice, the argument put forward is complex and difficult to follow without prior knowledge of this theory base.

****

Text/Book: Kadushin, A. and Kadushin, G. (1997) *The social work interview* (4th edn), New York, NY: Columbia University Press[56]
Country: USA
Overview: This text sees the interview as a special form of communication. It argues that in order to understand the social work interview, students and practitioners need to gain a more general understanding of the process of communication. This involves looking at the importance of questions and questioning techniques, listening skills, non-verbal communication and cross-cultural interviewing skills, such as the skills required when working with interpreters and how to work effectively and sensitively with people with hearing impairments. Problem-solving interventions are also covered, together with a chapter on 'problematic interviews', such as those involving involuntary clients or children who have been sexually abused. Some language used in this text would not be the more sensitive terminology used in most UK social work courses and like most texts from the US, it is written primarily for a North American audience.

Paper: Koprowska, J. (2003) 'The right kind of telling? Locating the teaching of interview skills with a systems framework', *British Journal of Social Work*, vol 22, pp 291-308[60]

Country: UK

Overview: This paper addresses the teaching and learning of interviewing skills on a social work course. The paper focuses on a model of professional education informed by Agazarian's theoretical framework of systems-centred therapy. This model identifies the obstacles to and opportunities for learning, and applies them to a skills module that addresses several core skills: attentive listening, empathy, clarification, challenging, goal setting and working with difference. The paper concludes with some suggestions for further research, several of which relate to the issue of the transferability and sustainability of skills learning in the practice context.

****

Text/Book: Lishman, J. (1994) *Communication in social work*, Basingstoke: Macmillan/BASW[62]

Country: UK

Overview: This is the only text reviewed specifically devoted to communication in social work. It provides a theoretical overview that refers to social psychology and behaviourism, and places particular emphasis on the importance of practice theory derived from professional experience and the client's (service user's) perspective. The text considers the relationship with the client (service user) to be central to effective practice and the core professional characteristics – genuineness, warmth, acceptance, encouragement, empathy and responsiveness – which contribute to effective communication skills. While addressing important aspects of communication skills, this book does not provide an explicit teaching programme relating to how the necessary skills can be taught and learnt.

****

Paper: MacFadden, R., Maiter, S. and Dumbrill, G. (2002) 'The high tech and high touch: the human face of online education', *Journal of Technology in Human Services*, vol 20, no 3/4, pp 283–300[64]

Country: Canada

Overview: This paper describes and evaluates the 'emotional topography' of e-learning from a student and a facilitator's perspective by exploring what it is like to be an e-learner. It emphasises the importance of concentrating on the emotional needs of an e-learner: for example, the need to ensure early success with the program, to reduce anxiety levels, and to avoid the learner getting lost in cyberspace. It contains a great deal of valuable guidance for people developing computer-based learning developers, which is translatable into a UK context.

****

Text/Book: Marsh, P. and Triseliotis, J. (1996) *Ready to practise? Social workers and probation officers: Their training and first year at work*, Aldershot: Avebury[66]
Country: UK
Overview: This important research looked at the structure and content of social work courses, and the extent to which this training prepared newly qualified social workers and probation offers for practice during their first year of employment. The study is based on data gathered from a sample of 714 newly qualified practitioners and 69 supervisors of newly qualified staff, and later data gathered from interviews with 60 newly trained social workers who qualified in 1994. While recognising the strengths of social work education, the authors highlighted a range of 'significant problems: "There is too much poor teaching in class, in placement and in first year training and support, especially regarding theoretical material and its application"[244] (A number of recommendations were put forward, including the suggestion that more attention needs to be given to the teaching of social work skills, using concrete practice examples and situations[245]).

****

Paper: Moss, B. (2000) 'The use of large-group role-play techniques in social work education', *Social Work Education*, vol 19, no 53, pp 471-83[71]
Country: UK
Overview: This paper provides a detailed account of the use of 'large-group role-play' to produce a learning environment which enables social work students to explore both structural and personal issues and dilemmas. There is a helpful discussion of the strengths of this approach, as a

preparation for practice learning, together with ways to tackle the pedagogical challenges it presents.

****

Paper: Nerdrum, P. and Lundquist, K. (1995) 'Does participation in communication skills increase student levels of communicated empathy? A controlled outcome study', *Journal of Teaching in Social Work*, vol 12, no 1/2, pp 139-57[74]
Country: Norway
Overview: This paper investigates whether social work students can increase their average level of empathic communication through participation in a specialised training course in communication skills. The authors found a significant difference after training between the programme group (39 students who undertook an intensive 11-week course) and the control group (39 students who received no systematic communication training). The paper has a useful discussion of the methodological challenges of measuring empathic communication.

****

Paper: Nerdrum, P. (1996) 'Steps towards an integration of basic therapeutic skills: a qualitative study of the development of the ideas of 15 social work students about being helpful to clients', *Scandinavian Journal of Social Welfare*, vol 5, pp 175-84[72]
Country: Norway
Overview: This paper describes a qualitative analysis of written proposals for helpful answers for 10 video-taped client situations, produced by 15 students before and after participation in the communication skills training course described in Nerdrum and Lundquist[74]. It provides an illuminating description of the development of the steps of skilfulness, and suggests that such development is slow and dependent on specific training of therapeutic skills.

****

Text/Book: Robinson, L. (1998) *Race: Communication and the caring professions*, Buckingham: Open University Press[81]
Country: UK

Overview: This book looks at current social work and healthcare literature in relation to inter-ethnic communication. In particular, it explores inter-ethnic communication from a Black perspective, and the way that prejudice and stereotypes act as barriers to effective communication between Black clients (service users), social workers and other healthcare professionals. An important feature of this text is the emphasis given to defining such terms as 'race', 'culture', 'identity', and why these terms are important when working with Black clients. It also looks at how to communicate effectively when working with Black clients who may not speak English or have English as a second language.

****

Text/Book: Thompson, N. (2002) *People skills: A guide to effective practice in the human services*, Basingstoke: Palgrave[92]
Country: UK
Overview: This text looks at the complex skills required when working with people from a range of diverse backgrounds and areas of need. Of particular relevance is Part Two on 'Interaction skills', which looks at such themes as valuing diversity, verbal communication, non-verbal communication, written communication, interviewing, influencing skills, handling feelings and handling conflict. In relation to teaching and learning, exercises are provided throughout the text that can be useful for teaching purposes. There is also a brief section entitled a 'Guide for tutors and trainers' that aims to help to apply theory to practice. Although popular among social work students, the text is designed to cover a broad range of occupations in the field of health and social care. As such, some topics are quite general and do not deal specifically with the kind of problems regularly encountered in a social work context.

****

Text/Book: Trevithick, P. (2000) *Social work skills: A practice handbook*, Buckingham: Open University Press[94]
Country: UK
Overview: This book examines 50 core skills used in social work practice. From the outset, Trevithick emphasises the importance of attention being paid to the theoretical frameworks and research evidence underpinning the teaching and learning communication skills. Without these

foundations, she suggests, the effectiveness of skills teaching and learning will be impaired. The early chapters of the book address this concern first, by exploring the nature of theory and its complex relationship with practice and, second, by examining different theoretical perspectives on human behaviour. The body of the book focuses on 50 social work skills which are broadly grouped into four categories: communication, listening and assessment skills; interviewing skills; skills required to help, direct and guide service users; and empowerment, negotiation and partnership skills. While it does not offer a specific approach to the teaching of these skills, the applied nature of the material and practice examples provide a firm foundation on which individual learning can be transposed and from which it can be developed.

****

APPENDIX C

Glossary of terms

Communication

Kadushin and Kadushin (1997)[56] provide a useful general description of the importance of communication:

> Communication is the sharing of thoughts, feelings, attitudes, and ideas through the exchange of verbal and nonverbal symbols. We share our private thoughts and feelings with others through communication. The work derives from *communicare*, the Latin verb that means to 'make common'.[246]

Pierson and Thomas (2000)[14] highlight the importance of communication in social work in detail:

> In social work and social welfare agencies, good, clear, accurate communication is essential in several contexts. First, all organizations should provide quality information about services that they offer, which should be widely accessible. This will involve not only a range of languages relevant to their local community but also in electronic, Braille and perhaps taped formats.

> Secondly, all workers need to develop appropriate communication skills both for face-to-face and for written communications. The ability to avoid jargon and to communicate in good, clear English and Welsh is of paramount importance. When using other languages, it is equally important that the clear meaning is fully communicated. Workers also need to consider the context in which they are required to speak and to write, and to ensure that they develop a style that is appropriate and relevant for their audience.

Thirdly, some people have specific communication needs. People who take pride in belonging to the deaf community, for example, need to be offered trained competent British Sign Language (BSL) interpreters so that they can communicate clearly in their first language. Some people who have serious communication problems as a result of disability may require specialist support for communication (see Braille, low-vision aids, Moon).

Fourthly, agencies that are closely collaborating on projects, working in partnership or negotiating service level agreements need to develop effective channels for communication in order to enhance collaboration.

Fifthly, with the developing emphasis upon a research culture in social welfare, workers need to be able to communicate clearly with funders, research colleagues and research participants in order to produce high quality results and be able to disseminate their findings clearly and imaginatively in order to improve practice.

Finally, communication has a non-verbal dimension. Workers need to be aware of body language, and the importance of listening skills, as part of their effective communication repertoire.[14]

Communication theory

Communication theory is most commonly associated with systems thinking. *Communication* relates to the sharing of meaningful interactions with other people in the world. It concerns the passing of, receiving and acting on information.

The theory examines the processes that communication involves: the selection of a means of conveying a message (language, gesture, writing), the decoding of the message by the recipient (hearing, seeing, reading), and making a response on the basis of the interpretation (reply). Understanding the rules and structures of communication can help to formulate sensitive and appropriate professional interactions with the service user.[247]

Competences

The General Social Care Council (GSCC) replaced the Central Council for Education and Training in Social Work (CCETSW) in 2001 but retained the same six competences required under the CCETSW's *Rules and regulations*. These 'core competences' include:

- communicate and engage
- promote and enable
- assess and plan
- intervene and provide services
- work in organisations
- develop personal competence.

The GSCC defines competence as follows:

> Competence in social work is the product of knowledge, skills and values. In order to provide evidence that they have achieved the six core competences students will have to demonstrate that they have: met practice requirements; integrated social work values; acquired and applied knowledge; reflected upon and critically analysed their practice; and transferred knowledge, skills and values in practice.[248]

NAW stipulate similar competence requirements in the *Requirements for an award of a degree in social work*. "Students must demonstrate progression through out the course of their degree and therefore must provide evidence of developing cumulative knowledge, competence and skills"[249].

Core skills

Core skills describe the foundation skills that are fundamental to effective practice in all social work contexts. These contexts cover a range of situations that can be categorised as involving work with individuals, families, carers, groups, communities, organisations and political structures. These core skills form a foundation for the development of generalist skills, and more advanced and specialist skills. However, effective practice is not solely dependent on the expertise of social workers, although centrally important. It is also dependent on the capacities of service users, and the wider environment, and how these are represented in the encounter. Therefore, effectiveness – in terms of competence and positive outcomes – is more likely to take place where practitioners are able to draw on their own capacities, and to relate these to the capacities, strengths and limitations, recognised in relation to service users and the wider environment. In general terms, these six core skills can be thought to include:

- observation and recognition skills;
- listening skills;
- communication skills: this includes verbal and non-verbal forms of communication, use of language, the written word; interviewing skills, information gathering and investigative skills;
- analytic skills: the ability to "acquire, critically evaluate, apply and integrate knowledge and understanding" to form a judgement (critical thinking)[250];
- decision making and assessment skills: the ability to analyse and apply theory, research and theorised practice knowledge to real life social work contexts;
- action skills: the ability to intervene in ways that influence beliefs, thoughts, feelings, and events. This involves drawing on a range of social work skills and practice approaches, based on an analysis of the data, practice experience and on a well-informed and integrated knowledge of theory and research.[251]

See also **Generalist skills**, **Macro-skills**, **Micro-skills**, and **Specialist skills or practice**.

Empathy

In order to be empathic, the worker has to be able to enter his/her client's subjective world, to feel what it might be like for the client, to understand what s/he might be thinking, and to convey this understanding back to the client. The worker has to be able to do this without taking on the client's internal world as his own. That is, I have to be able to understand my client's confusion without becoming confused myself.[252]

Importance of self-knowledge in relation to empathy: the capacity to be in touch with the client's feelings is related to the worker's ability to acknowledge his or her own. Before a worker can understand the power of emotion in the life of the client, it is necessary to discover its importance in the worker's own experience.[253]

Empowerment

There has been an explosion of interest in the idea of empowerment in social care. This reflects broader interest in a concept which transcends conventional politics and ideology, addresses both the *personal* and the *political*, and seeks to unite the two. Empowerment has become a key concept in social work and social care. It is now central in political, social policy, educational, cultural, sexual, personal and managerial discourses, as well as entering popular usage. At the same time, there are concerns among social care service users and professionals that the term has been reduced to jargon through over-use and lack of clarity.[254]

Barker's definition of empowerment: in social work practice, the process of helping individuals, families, groups and communities increase their personal, interpersonal, socioeconomic, and political strength and influence toward improving their circumstances.[255]

Evaluation of effectiveness

The evaluation of effectiveness involves measuring the outcomes of social work intervention against its objectives. Such an endeavour is critical to the development of evidence-based social work policy and practice.[256]

Evidence-based practice

Evidence based practice denotes an approach to decision making which is transparent, accountable, and based on a consideration of current best evidence about the effects of particular interventions on the welfare of individuals, groups and communities. It relates to the decisions of both individual practitioners and policy makers.[257]

Generalist skills

A social work practitioner whose knowledge and skills encompass a broad spectrum and who assess problems and their solutions comprehensively. The generalist often co-ordinates the efforts of specialists by facilitating communication between them, thereby fostering continuity of care.[258]

Generic social work

The social work orientation that emphasises a common core of knowledge and skills associated with social service delivery. A generic social worker possesses basic knowledge that may span several methods in social work. Such a social worker would not necessarily be a specialist in a single field of practice or professional technique but would be capable of providing and managing a wider range of needed client services and intervening in a greater variety of systems.[259]

Generic social work assumes a common core of knowledge, values and skills underpinning all practice.[260]

See also **Core skills, Macro–skills, Micro–skills** and **Specialist skills or practice**.

Interpretation

Interpretations often refer to material expressed only implicitly. In this way, they differ from listening responses. This view of interpretation is similar to Egan's advanced accurate empathy. Interpretations may help clients understand relationships between events, consider behaviour from a different perspective, and act more effectively in real life.... Try to avoid premature interpretations and suggestions.[261]

Intervention

The word 'intervention' means *coming between* (derived from the Latin inter: *between* and venire: *to come*). A dictionary definition states taking "a decisive or intrusive role in order to modify or determine events or their outcome" (*Collins English Dictionary*). According to Kennard et al:

> Interventions inevitably make up a substantial majority of human behaviour. They are made by those who desire and intend to influence some part of the world and the beings within it.[262]

Barker's definition of intervention
1. Interceding or coming between groups of people, events, planning activities, or an individual's internal conflicts. 2. In social work, the term is analogous to the physician's term *treatment*. Many social workers prefer using 'intervention' because it includes 'treatment' and also encompasses the other activities social workers use to solve or prevent problems or achieve goals for social betterment.[263]

Interviewing

> An interview is a specialised form of communication.... [It] involves two people, each of whom possesses a receiving system, a processing system, and a transmitting system.[246]

We can describe the general purposes of most social work interviews as informational (to make a social study), assessment (to arrive at an understanding), and therapeutic (to effect change). These are discrete categories only for the purpose of analysis; the same interview can, and often does, serve more than one purpose.[264]

Social workers spend more time interviewing than any other single activity
Although social work involves a great deal more than interviewing, social workers spend more time in interviewing than in any other single activity.... This is most clearly true of the direct service worker.

But the group worker and community organiser also frequently participate in interviewing.[265]

Knowledge underpinning social work

The knowledge underpinning social work practice derives from many different sources. Competent practice will depend upon knowledge of law, social policy, philosophy (ethics), sociology, social administration, organisational policies, procedures and guidelines, numerous theories, differing social work methods.[266]

Language

Language is the essential medium of all social influence and intervention. Social workers should use language that is clear, accessible and informative. Clients are not best helped by workers who use obscure, inaccurate, deceptive or demeaning language. Professionals are less effective on their clients' behalf if they cannot communicate precisely and persuasively.[267]

Language informs the way we think, the way we experience, and the way we interact with each other. Language provides the basis of community, but also the grounds for division. Systematic knowledge about language and practical awareness of how it works is fundamental to the process of building mature communities.[268]

Learning

Under the main heading 'Learning, teaching and assessment', the benchmarking statement[269] describes the learning processes in social work in terms of four interrelated themes:

- *awareness raising and knowledge acquisition:* a process in which a student becomes more aware of aspects of knowledge and expertise, engages with and acquires new areas of knowledge, recognises their potential and becomes motivated to engage in new ways of thinking and acting;

- *conceptual understanding:* a process in which a student acquires, examines critically and deepens understanding (measured and tested against existing knowledge and adjustments made in attitudes and goals);
- *practice experience:* processes in which a student applies theoretical models together with new understanding and skills to relevant activities and receives feedback on performance enhancing openness to critical self-evaluation;
- *reflection on performance:* a process in which a student reflects on past experience, recent performance, and feedback, and applies this information to the process of integrating awareness (including awareness of the impact of self on others) and new understanding, leading to improved performance.

Kolb emphasises the transformational nature of learning and its relationship to knowledge:
Learning *is the process whereby knowledge is created through the* transformation of *experience.* This definition emphasises several critical aspects of the learning process as viewed from the experiential perspective. First is the emphasis on the process of adaptation and learning as opposed to content or outcomes. Second is that knowledge is a transformation process, being continuously created and recreated, not an independent entity to be acquired or transmitted. Third, learning transforms experience in both its objective and subjective forms. Finally, to understand learning, we must understand the nature of knowledge, and vice versa.[270]

According to Kolb, "Knowledge results from the combination of grasping experience and transforming it".[271]

Listening

Listening refers to the ability of helpers to capture and understand the messages clients communicate, whether these messages are transmitted verbally or nonverbally, clearly or vaguely.[272]

Listening versus hearing

Kadushin and Kadushin (1997)[56] differentiate between the two by describing hearing as a *physiological act* – the appreciation of sound – whereas listening is seen as a *cerebral act* – that of understanding[273]. We may hear what is being said, but this could be a passive activity while listening requires a more active involvement. "People want more than physical presence in human communication; they want the other person to be present psychologically, socially, and emotionally".[274]

Macro-skills

'Macro-skills' is a term commonly used in North American social work to describe the skills used where the focus is on attempting to initiate change in the wider societal context, particularly political, economic, and environmental elements that impact on people in ways that influence the quality of their lives and the opportunities to bring about change:

> Such activities include some types of political action, community organization, public education campaigning, and the administration of broad-based social services agencies or public welfare departments.[275]

Micro-skills

This term is used to describe the skills and interventions used when working directly with people, rather than the wider societal context. Barker defines micro-skills as:

> The term used by social workers to identify professional activities that are designated to help solve the problems faced primarily by individuals, families and social groups. Usually micro practice focuses on direct interventions on a case-by-case basis or in a clinical setting.[276]

See also **Generalist skills**, **Macro-skills**, **Micro-skills**, and **Specialist skills or practice**.

Non-verbal communication

Non-verbal communication can be broadly divided into two area: proxemics concerned with distance and how close people like to be to each other and kinesics referring to movements, gestures, expression and eye contact. More simply we can consider the following areas: distance, posture and orientation, gaze and eye contact, and facial expression.[277]

For Kadushin and Kadushin, non-verbal communication includes:

1. chronomics (time keeping)
2. artifactual communication (personal attire/dress)
3. smell (body odours)
4. touch (handshaking, hugs)
5. paralinguistic (how words are said in terms of their tone, pitch, volume, speed, emphasis, intonation, articulation and intensity)
6. proxemics (space and distance)
7. body language-kinesics (movement, gesture and body posture particularly in relation to the eyes, face, hands, legs and feet).[278]

Important communications represented in body language

Detailed studies have identified many items in the nonverbal vocabulary, including five thousand distinctly different hand gestures have been identified and one thousand different steady body postures. Precise observation of nonverbal behaviour is important, but it is only a first step. The interviewer still has to infer some valid meaning from the data. Accurate observation is necessary but insufficient for understanding the psychological relevance of the gesture.[279]

Observation

In the benchmarking statement, activities such as observation are related to practice learning and the importance of actively engaging with service users[250]. Gambrill stresses its importance:

Observation in real-life settings may be required to clarify problems and identify related circumstances. Without a fine-grained (detailed) description of problem-related contingencies based on careful observation, you may make inaccurate assumptions about maintaining conditions. You may overlook problem-related behaviours of misapplied and unapplied contingencies. Each individual is unique. Only through careful observation may interaction patterns between clients and significant others be understood.[280]

Problem-solving skills

Under the heading 'Subject skills and other skills'[281], the Social Work benchmarking statement places important emphasis on problem-solving skills and sub-divides these into **four** areas:

3.2.2.1   Managing problem-solving activities
3.2.2.2   Gathering information
3.2.2.3   Analysis and synthesis
3.2.2.4   Intervention and evaluation.[281]

> **Gambrill links problem-solving skills to critical thinking:**
> Successful compared to unsuccessful problem solvers think more about their thinking. They critically review their assumptions and reasoning. They are their own best critics. They ask questions about the accuracy of data. They ask: What evidence supports this claim? Has it been critically tested? With what results? Are their plausible alternative views?[282]

Skills (social work skills or practice skills)

Under the heading 'Subject skills and other skills'[281], the benchmarking statement states that "Social work honours graduates should acquire and integrate skills in **five core areas**". These include:

3.2.1   Communication and InformationTechnology (C&IT) and numerical skills

3.2.2   Problem solving skills

3.2.3   Communication skills

3.2.4   Skills in working with others

3.2.5   Skills in personal and professional development.

Cournoyer defines social work skills as:

… a circumscribed set of discrete cognitive and behavioural actions that (1) derive from social work knowledge and from social work values, ethics, and obligations; (2) are consistent with the essential facilitative qualities; (3) reflect the characteristics of professional integrity; and (4) comport with a social work purpose within the context of a phase or process of practice.[283]

Barker describes 'direct practice skills' as:

The ability to put social work knowledge into effective intervention activities with individuals, families, groups and communities.[284]

See also **Core skills, Macro-skills, Micro-skills, Generalist skills** and **Specialist skills or practice**.

Specialist skills or practice

Parsloe sees specialist practice as indicating "either a division of labour or superior knowledge and skill about a client group, problem area, methods or settings"[260]. Thus, the skills demonstrated by social work practitioners using specialist skills could include significant knowledge and experience applying, say, cognitive behavioural techniques, such as systematic desensitisation, contingent management[285] and so on. Or the specialist skills might relate to the use of specific skills in relation to a particular client group, such as the use of Macaton with people with learning difficulties or particular expertise in a given area of practice, such as the skills required to work with bereavement and loss. Specialist skills imply a degree of practice experience and knowledge, and that additional training has been undertaken.

The specialist practitioner can be at the front line or specialism can extend up the organization.... There has been little research into whether the different practices have different outcomes. A question, of particular relevance for social work education, concerns the stage at which social workers should specialize.[260]

Teaching (or learning methods)

Under the main heading 'Learning, teaching, and assessment' (4.1), the benchmarking statement acknowledges that adults learn at different rates and in diverse ways which, therefore, require teachers to provide a range of learning and teaching strategies. These different learning methods may include:

- student-focused approaches that encourage active participation and staged, progressive learning throughout the degree;
- the establishment of initial learning needs and the formulation of learning plans;
- the development of resource networks, enabling students to learn from each other;
- lectures, role plays, case presentations, individual and group practice experience, simulations, investigative group projects, skills learning assisted by CCTV and video-recording, seminars, presentation of practice studies;
- the use of communication and information technology systems for accessing data, literature, resources, and contacts.[286]

Theory/social work theory

Under the heading 'Social work theory', the benchmarking statement identifies the range of theories and perspectives to be taught on social work courses. These include:

- Research-based concepts and critical explanations from social work theory and other disciplines that contribute to the knowledge base of social work, including their distinctive epistemological status and application to practice.

- The relevance of sociological perspectives to understanding societal and structural influences on human behaviour at individual, group and community levels.
- The relevance of psychological and physiological perspectives to understanding individual and social development and functioning.
- Social science theories explaining group and organisational behaviour, adaptation and change.
- Models and methods of assessment, including factors underpinning the selection and testing of relevant information, the nature of professional judgement and the processes of risk assessment.
- Approaches and methods of intervention in a range of community-based settings including group-care at individual, group and community levels, including factors guiding the choice and evaluation of these.
- Knowledge and critical appraisal of relevant social research and evaluation methodologies.[286]

For Barker, theory is defined as:
A group of related hypotheses, concepts, and constructs, based on facts and observations, that attempts to explain a particular phenomenon.[287]

Transferability of skills

Learning and perfecting social work skills to the point that they are transferable, that is, reliable and enduring even under difficult, if not impossible, situations is a life-long learning process[288]. The same is true of the ability to transfer skills and knowledge across different groups, and social work settings and circumstances. Central to the ability to transfer skills and knowledge is the ability to link theory to practice – it is this capacity that removes a 'hit and miss' approach to practice delivery. This theoretical understanding includes a sound knowledge of psychology and sociology, combined with an understanding of the uniqueness of every human being and experience[289]. It also involves being able to use the findings of research in ways that are reflective and demonstrate the capacity for critical thinking.

Gambrill describes transferability as 'translation skills':
In the United States, the transferability of skills is sometimes called 'translation skills'. 'To discover options, we may have to translate concepts from one discipline to another or combine them in a way that yields a more comprehensive whole and does not contain contradictory assumptions'.[290]

Index

Note: Page numbers followed by *bib* refer to entries in the *Annotated bibliography* in Appendix B; page numbers followed by *glos* refer to entries in the *Glossary of terms* in Appendix C.

core skills 1, 2, 110-11, 115-16*glos*,
124-5
see also communication skills;
interpersonal skills; interviewing
skills; listening skills
counselling
'micro-counselling' skills 14, 20-1,
22, 24
teaching communication skills 20
telephone technology 30-1
theories of 12, 13-14, 18
Cournoyer, B. 17, 25, 104*bib*, 125
crisis intervention theory 12
critical thinking 104, 116, 124, 127
cross-cultural practice 30
see also transcultural
communication

D
Dawson, R.D. 24
decision making skills 116
Dept of Health (DH): core skills 1,
2
Dickson, D. 11-12, 17, 20-1, 22,
104-5*bib*
direct skills acquisition 16, 125
disabled people: communication
needs 3, 29
diversity and interpersonal skills
110
Dobson, S. 29
Dockar-Drysdale, B. 16
Dreher, B.-B. 29
Dreyfus, H. 16
Dreyfus, S. 16

E
e-learning *see* information
technology
Economic and Social Research
Council (ESRC) 31-2
Edwards, J.B. 15-16
effectiveness 117*glos*

Egan, G. 14, 66, 118
electronic database search 4, 7, 8,
59, 60-1, 65-7
empathy 13-14, 15-16, 116-17*glos*
skills laboratory training 26
in teaching communication skills
20, 109
empowerment 15, 117*glos*
Engen, H.B. 24
Erikson's stages 12
evaluation of effectiveness 117*glos*
evaluative accounts of teaching
communication skills 5, 19,
20-3, 27, 34-5, 37-8, 104-5
lacking for special needs
communication 31
literature search results 68-9
Evans, D.R. 25
evidence-based practice 117-18*glos*
experiential focusing 20
experiential learning 15, 20
IT-based approaches 24

F
face-to-face communication skills
3
feedback, systematic 20
Fieweger, M.A. 30
Fischer, J. 13
Foucault, Michel 16
Freire, P. 16
Freudian theory 13

G
Gambrill, E. 123-4
General Social Care Council
(GSCC) 2, 115
generalist skills 118*glos*
generic social work 118*glos*
glossary of terms 12, 113-28

limited literature on 11, 33, 37-8
literature search results 68-9
literature specific to social work
    17-18, 105-7
other theories 15-17, 106
psychology and counselling
    theories 13-14
and teaching communications
    skills 12-13, 39-40, 105, 110-11
IT-based learning 24
Thomas, M. 3, 113-14
Thompson, N. 18, 25, 110*bib*
Thurman, S. 29
Toseland, R. 20
transcultural communication 30,
    35-6, 37, 109-10
transferability of skills 34-5, 40,
    104-5, 127-8*glos*
Brunel Practice Survey 17, 35, 37
laboratory-based skills 22, 26-7,
    37-8, 103
lack of research on 34
translation skills 128
Trevithick, P. 18, 110-11*bib*
Triseliotis, J. 37, 108*bib*

U
user involvement 3, 16-17, 35, 37

V
videotape training 16, 20, 23-4, 26,
    109
Vinton, L. 26

W
Webster, B.J. 30
Welsh language 35-6
Winnicott, D. 16
women with special
    communication needs 29-30
Working Group 1-2, 4-5
written communication skills 3, 19,
    27

Z
Zapf, M.K. 30

Other knowledge reviews available from SCIE

KNOWLEDGE REVIEW 1
Learning and teaching in social work education: Assessment
Beth R. Crisp, Mark R. Anderson, Joan Orme and Pam Green Lister
1 904812 00 7
November 2003

KNOWLEDGE REVIEW 2
The adoption of looked after children: A scoping review of research
Alan Rushton
1 904812 01 5
November 2003

KNOWLEDGE REVIEW 3
Types and quality of knowledge in social care
Ray Pawson, Annette Boaz, Lesley Grayson, Andrew Long and Colin Barnes
1 904812 02 3
November 2003

KNOWLEDGE REVIEW 4
Innovative, tried and tested: A review of good practice in fostering
Clive Sellick and Darren Howell
1 904812 03 1
November 2003

KNOWLEDGE REVIEW 5
Fostering success: An exploration of the research literature in foster care
Kate Wilson, Ian Sinclair, Claire Taylor, Andrew Pithouse and Clive Sellick
1 904812 04 X
January 2004